"You are holding in your hands the book: *Understanding is the New Healing*. You did not pick up this book by chance. Perhaps it is an answer to an unspoken question you have been asking about your Soul's unfoldment, past lives, sacred wisdom and receptivity to Divine guidance. If those questions have been reverberating somewhere in your awareness, this book may be a part of that answer. Through personal stories of healing and release of cellular memories that have blocked the flow of happiness and great reflections on insights regarding universal principles, you'll be ushered into greater clarity and well-being. Dr. Mary Helen Hensley has woven together an extraordinary volume of spiritual inspiration that will bring great understanding and great healing. Read it and watch your life change for the better."

—Richest Blessings, Michael Bernard Beckwith
Founder & Spiritual Director, Agape International Spiritual Center.
Author, *Life Visioning and Spiritual Liberation*

"Sharing wisdom after having extensive experiences with the profound gifts received during the transition from life to death. An invaluable blessing to those struggling to make sense of such events, many will realize that the gift of knowing our eternal connection with loved ones is beautifully supported when we share the dying process."

—Eben Alexander MD, neurosurgeon and author of *Living in a Mindful Universe* and *Proof of Heaven*

"A spell-binding and compelling read, will keep you on the edge of your seat and break your heart open."

—Tosha Silver, author of *Outrageous Openness* and *Change Me Prayers*

"How do you explain Mary Helen Hensley? Yes, she came into this life a gifted child. Yes, she had a near-death experience that opened her up to worlds beyond this one. Yes, she is a doctor, healer, a metaphysical counselor, a medium, a seer between worlds. Mary Helen has discovered a secret. It's not the what or why or how or when of life that heals. It's understanding. What difference does it make if your problem can be traced to a past life, or if your breast cancer means the end of this one? Nestled at our very core, all of us, is the measure to our healing...that grace point between soul and personality where we confront the why between choice and result. Mary Helen takes us there via humorous tales of her own life, her mistakes, her patients and what they discovered. The honesty, the heart-stopping proof of success in this one book, is unlike anything else I have ever read. A real treasure!"

—P.M.H. Atwater L.H.D., near-death researcher and author of such books as *A Manual for Developing Humans, Future Memory Children of the Fifth World, Dying to Know You: Proof of God in the Near Death Experience* and *Near-Death Experiences: The Rest of the Story*

"*Understanding is the New Healing* will open you to different possibilities and a way of thinking that will bring comfort and understanding of all of life's difficulties. A very thought provoking and ultimately life changing read."

—Patricia Scanlan, International Best-selling Author

UNDERSTANDING
IS THE
NEW HEALING

BY
DR. MARY HELEN HENSLEY

I dedicate this book to the physician who never sleeps,

Dr. Garland H. Clark. In life and until his dying day, my

grandfather, 'Judge' helped so many, with his kind heart and

healing hands. Beyond death, his legacy continues to serve

mankind. He was my very first friend and gave me his word

that he'd never leave my side.

Thanks for keeping your promise.

I love you.

CONTENTS

Dear Friends,

As a curious, young girl growing up in the foothills of the Blue Ridge Mountains of Virginia, there was never a shortage of great books in my home. Really, when I think back, how could I *not* have become an author? My father was always perched at the head of the kitchen table, writing speeches, sermons and eulogies, with books piled around him for reference, while my mother grabbed every spare moment to nestle into her favourite turquoise arm chair, to complete the latest assignment for one of the several book clubs to which she belonged. The book shelves throughout the house were stuffed to the brim with volumes of self-help and positive living titles, religious and historical texts, and of course, Mom's very favourite, the murder mysteries. It was as good as living in the public library. One book, however, really sticks out in my mind as a staple in our household collection.

Ever so proud of her Kentucky roots, my mother's favourite book was always visible around the house, with a threadbare cover and well-worn pages from decades of reading it over and over again... as if for the very first time. It's not the content that stays with me all of these years later, ***but the title.***

"The Thread That Runs So True" is the personal account of Jesse Stuart, a teacher in the mountainous region of the state of Kentucky. First published in 1949, it became a classic amongst generations of teachers and students alike, with witty and often daunting tales of the challenges of teaching in a one-room schoolhouse in the rural South. I remember reading the book because I knew it would make my mother happy. Little did she know that its title would one day be used to explain intricate metaphysical concepts in her daughter's eighth book.

My mother's father, Dr. Garland Clark, was a family doctor and surgeon in Winchester, Kentucky, until his death, when I was only one. Fifty years later, as a doctor, metaphysician and author myself, the passion for life and awe for death that my grandfather instilled in me while growing up seems the most appropriate way to introduce the stories I am about to share. *Wait a minute! Didn't she just say he died when she was one?* I can see you scratching your heads... He did. It was beyond his physical death, in 1970, that I forged a lasting relationship with this man affectionately known by my family as 'Judge'.

My earliest memories are of conversations with Judge, as real and meaningful as any I have ever had with anyone *in a body*. Doc Clark would come to me at night, often telling me fantastic stories, parables of sorts, explaining to me that I was here to be of service to mankind, just as he had been. While no one had ever spoken of his healing abilities outside of his role as a medical doctor until *after* his passing, he assured me that I would be sharing my gifts in a much more tangible and communal way. In essence, I would eventually be telling both of our stories, with the aim of setting people free, 'letting them off the hook', as such, and reminding them that the power to heal is in each and every one of us if we can quiet our minds long enough to truly understand the issues in our tissues. They were meaty conversations for a little kid, but I always took them in my stride. I depended on Judge's counsel to get me through my formative years; a time when the only people I could talk to about my prophetic dreams and visions were my mom and dad. While they always did their best to attempt to understand me, they were deeply ensconced in their practice of the modern Christian faith and often struggled with my incredibly detailed reports of the great beyond. My father advised that we keep these things between us, while my mother was secretly delighted to know that not only was her own beloved father alive and well in spirit, he was somehow able to communicate with her youngest child. He has remained my closest advisor throughout my entire life, an existence that I have dedicated to our mutual cause; reminding anyone who will listen that **we already are that which we seek**.

One might ask, what does this have to do with Jesse Stuart's classic book, "The Thread That Runs So True"? As I said before, it's all in the title. One of the many metaphysical principals taught to me by my grandfather in spirit, is the concept that lifetimes are like a thread…*a thread that runs so true.* It's simple, really. When a soul chooses to incarnate on planet Earth, temporarily leaving behind the all-knowing, all-loving omnipotence of the Divine Presence, it's very like going off to a University. When we embark on tertiary education, we choose a course of study, declare a major and then proceed to take every class on offer, in order to achieve the most -well-rounded education pertaining to the dedicated subject. If it's art, we don't just take one drawing class and declare ourselves a master at the craft. We take drawing, art appreciation, sculpture, painting, art throughout history, European and African art, American art, graphic design, art in social media, and the list goes on. At the end of the degree, hopefully we graduate with a firm grasp of art that can assist with the next phase of life; the application of the knowledge we have acquired, in both a personal and professional capacity.

Lifetimes on Earth, run a very similar pattern. There is a thread, a series of incarnations that follow an outline, maximising the opportunity for a soul to **own** a spiritual concept using the body as the vehicle in which to navigate the incarnation. The thread will see a soul take on a theme, choosing circumstances that will best support the final outcome of total knowing of a subject, emotion or feeling which is unique to the human experience. If the soul wishes to know compassion, it may incarnate into a lifetime that shows it *anything but* compassion. Subsequently, *or simultaneously,* if the truth be told, a soul will build on the lessons in a series of lifetimes that will see it experience compassion as an observer, a participant, a facilitator, an aggressor, etc. It's not like climbing a staircase to enlightenment, or riding a one-way train, but more like hopping aboard a merry-go-round in order to take in the full view all at once.

The easiest way to explain threads of life is to have you visualise north, south, east and west. For example, when that merry-go-round passes north, a woman is there, smiling and waving at you. When it spins past east, there is a man serving cones from an ice-cream truck. When it sails through south, a dog sits panting, maybe wagging its tail. When it circles around to the west, children are splashing in a fountain. With each 360 degrees turn, four completely different scenarios are playing out, yet all are being experienced during the same ride by you, the observer. Just because the woman is waving from the north doesn't mean the dog isn't also wagging its tail in the south. Children laugh and play in the west as a man serves ice-cream at the exact same time in the east. It defies the linear concept of time marching forward and our threads of lifetimes now become an inter-twined series of loops. Many metaphysicians talk linear or chronological lifetimes when first introducing the concept of multiple lives, myself included, simply because it is easier to digest for those who are just discovering that this isn't their first and only rodeo here on Earth. The idea of a concurrent **Multiverse** of experiences as opposed to a singular lifetime in a **Universe** has the tendency to fry the circuits of folks who are new to metaphysics or have been pre-conditioned by religious institutions that promote duality as eternal as opposed to circumstantial. For those who live according to the Multiverse model, it's hard to sell an everlasting afterlife (courtesy of a messiah who rescues a soul from the mortal sins accrued in a single lifetime) to someone who embraces the notion of numerous lives and spiritual guidance from a myriad of avatars. To one who truly grasps this concept, it explains the role of the **numerous** loving masters who have walked this Earth for millennia. These beings of Love and Light do not come to be worshipped or to have religions created in their name, their intention is to be the embodiment of pure love in its true form; to support, guide and *remind* those who are so deeply ensconced in the human life cycles that they are *in it* but not *of it*. The free will which belongs to us all dictates how long or short the eventual return The Source will be, based on the knowledge and understanding created by these threads or loops of lifetimes.

Personally, I love it here. Following an encounter with death in a high-speed collision in 1991, which resulted in a prolonged and memorable experience in the 'space between lives' realm of the earthly experience (that many associate with Heaven), I have the wonderful blessing in my life of knowing from whence I came. I admit that this *knowing* certainly makes it a lot easier for me to weather the inevitable storms of being alive in the physical form. I'm not homesick. I'm here because I remember that I **chose** to be here. I know where home really is and I also know with every fibre of my being that no one can harm **the real me**. I don't waste a single moment of the gift of being human wishing I was 'out of here', because eventually *I will be.*

A combination of essential amnesia and razor sharp focus on the total embodiment of a character allows a soul to play out any given scenario of victim, victor, dastardly perpetrator or do-gooder via a spiritual truth that is based on frequency and vibration. Whatever is receiving the attention *or love* of the soul incarnate is what that soul temporarily *becomes.* There are schools of thought that take this theory from the 3D physical into the ethereal space between lives, suggesting that those who are coming from a hellish vibration or darker soul group will incarnate with this as their focal point; to harm, create chaos and literal hell on Earth for themselves and those with whom they interact. In my personal experience, I can resonate with many aspects of this, however, what I witnessed beyond the veil suggests that while on the surface a soul can appear purely evil, it's much like an athlete who keeps his 'game face' even when off the playing field or like an actor who remains in character when the cameras aren't rolling just to ensure authenticity. When a soul is in the frequency of the Earth realm, (which includes the reverberation of disincarnate souls 'in- between' lives, often mistaken as a 'final destination' such as Heaven), it stands to reason that those who are carrying a frequency of fear and separation will gather together because they are working on the same types of threads or lessons. In this space, souls actively integrate information from the incarnation cycles of this planet, sometimes remaining completely submerged in whatever role they have played (but will eventually move on from). For some, this can become a prolonged and indefinite reality. Ultimately, however, there is no soul that does not come from or return to the light in due time; the One True Source of All That Is.

Each lifetime within a thread is a fragment, a mere filament of the strand, as it takes many fibres to complete a simple piece of string. No one lifetime, no single piece of the thread is more or less important than another, and in turn, the thread ultimately weaves an intricate tapestry of lifetimes and experiences that allows the soul to truly know itself and what it means to be human. The body is merely a vehicle, the thread is the highway on which it travels and the end of the thread or series of incarnations is the complete understanding that brings our awareness back to the One True Love. As masters of the experiences we set out to create, we provide our own answers to the age old question…when speaking of infinity, just how long is a piece of string? Well…it's as long as we need it to be.

Inevitably there are those who will ask, "Why bother? If we come from the light, if we already are perfect to begin with, why would we put ourselves through the harrowing experience of being human in an excruciatingly painful world?" I'll attempt to explain this mind-bender in the simplest way I can. Picture a family with a state-of-the-art home entertainment centre which allows them to watch any movie on demand; the giant screen TV, the surround sound and HD explosion of vibrant colour and perfect sound. Why would the family ever bother going to the cinema? If they already have everything they need at home, why leave? It's warm and cosy, they can pause the movie for a bathroom break or a trip to the fully stocked fridge. If someone gets tired, they can record the movie and watch it later, at their convenience. What on Earth could possibly motivate them to go drop fifty bucks at the theatre when they can have it all in the comfort of their own home?

Now imagine the buzz of planning an outing with your family or friends; the anticipation of seeing the latest film on a massive screen on the day of its release, the air in the cinema heavy with the smell of buttery popcorn and chocolately sweets; the two hours that require all phones and technology to be switched off.

Hear the rousing laughter of an audience enjoying a good comedy, feel in your heart the palpable sorrow, the coughing and sniffling of the guy sitting next to you, as he attempts to hide public tears when a story-line tugs at his heart. Picture the chatter and critiques amongst friends after the show, ruminating over the likes and dislikes of captivating performances by old favourites and edgy new stars, delivering unexpected plot twists via incredible cinematic reveals.

Leaving the comforts of home for an external excursion is a concept to which any adrenaline junkie can easily relate. A soul, who knows its origins and is at one with its Divine and eternal nature, is going to look forward to its time on 'planet Earth' with great anticipation for *every* experience....the more challenging the better. It's only when we try to absorb this notion with our human minds that we trip ourselves up. When we are in the thick of adversity, it's difficult to imagine *choosing*, let alone being *excited* about personal hardship.

To know thyself; to throw caution to the wind and truly know thyself by shattering into millions of pieces, experiencing the world through the eyes of every possible perspective; this is why we come here. So many people who are suffering have looked me in the eyes and said, "I **never** would have chosen this and I'm certainly not ever coming back after I die." To endeavour to grasp the enormity of the perfectly perfect plan with a human mind and five senses is a daunting and more or less impossible task for most.

To embrace the idea that pain, suffering and heartache are scripts that we personally penned in order to push ourselves to the limits while here on Earth is a very perplexing vision to peddle to one who can't remember, or to another who has deeply personified their wounds. To suggest to someone that their greatest offenders, the individuals who have seemingly set out to destroy the life experience of others out of pure malice and cruelty, may in some way be serving them, is a tough sell on the best of days. The idea that a loving soul would agree to forget all of their inherent goodness and come to Earth to assist a fellow soul on a mission, by creating difficulty and pain, is unthinkable to those who are still working through the duality of good and evil; the 'us versus them' mentality of Heaven and Hell. What about accountability? Does this mean the 'bad guys' just get away with it? It's not as embryonic as that, folks. Allow me to clarify.

A young girl had a horrific experience with a school principal, who humiliated this child in front of her schoolmates in order to divert attention away from a serious bullying problem within the school system. In the blink of an eye, this twelve year old, who had been the target of appalling cruelty, became the subject of shame, as if she had been a troubled child seeking an audience. Rather than the school's administration protecting her from the daily, incessant attacks by a small group of her peers, they made her feel as if she was attention seeking by crying 'bully'. Feeling worthless and dejected, she attempted to take her own life. When her efforts failed, she began a long and arduous journey of self-discovery that took her to the darkest confines of her own mind, while her family seemingly could do nothing…nothing but love and support her, seek assistance for her and **trust** the bigger picture of her Divine plan.

This child and her family suffered and grew together, each one developing coping mechanisms with the skills that they already possessed and with the new tools that this situation was providing. There were many people, including the family members and friends of the individual who had emotionally abused this child, who had an entirely different experience of this 'educator'. Loving and kind, humorous and involved, their 'knowing' of this loved one was the polar opposite of the individual this girl and her family had endured. Conversations developed over time in the household of the child concerning inner strength and a deep sense of personal accountability to the source of one's happiness. The child was evolving in front of her family's eyes in to a thoughtful, introspective and wise young human being. The physical and emotional scars of her self-loathing were no longer covered. She accepted them and learned not to judge herself because of someone else's opinions or 'bad' behaviour. She eventually re-engaged with her friends, applied herself in school and spoke more openly about her feelings, thoughts, fears and desires. Her relationship with her family and with herself improved drastically. She often found herself 'counselling' her peers through the tough moments that the teen-age years have to offer. Her vision of who she wanted to be and what she wanted to become later in life began to come in to focus with a clarity she had never known. While her family had followed the appropriate channels to report the principal's wrong-doing, this child wanted it to go no further in *her own story*. She saw it for what it was and for her, that was enough. To one who is living the model of duality, desperate for justice, accountability and the punishment of the perpetrator, this story would not be complete until heads rolled in that school. For the child, the lesson had been immense, one that allowed her to find a personal strength and love that she never knew existed. The family and friends who know the 'educator' as nothing but wonderful and the family of the young girl who experienced this person as evil incarnate, all know the same person **simultaneously**. This woman became the cause **and** the effect in this young girl's greatest challenge to date.

So who is the 'educator'? On which merits should the 'educator' be judged? Do we discount the person's positive attributes because of the painful or do we overlook the painful because of the positive? We can't casually profess that **all things** are in the hands of God, only when it suits us, or that our darkest adversaries are somehow exempt from the loving plans of our Divine selves. There are gifts to be found in every interaction if we have the eyes to see them.

The very reason I write the extremely personal accounts on behalf of the generous souls who were willing to share their stories in this book, is so more people might catch the spark...the tiny ember of recollection that keeps burning in our hearts, pushing us forward with a willingness to believe that there is *something* far more Divine at work than our fear, hopes or inability to remember **the plan**.

Over the years, I have been blessed to facilitate the healing sessions of so many extraordinary human beings. These accounts are snapshots in time of the adventures in self-discovery of some of your fellow travellers on this glorious and diverse planet; the planet, which by design offers the dichotomy and duality of coexisting dark and light. My wish is that you may resonate with a few, finding similarities to your own life within. I encourage you to look beyond the facilitator; don't allow yourself to get hung up on what I do. I'm nothing more than a washer woman, scrubbing away the dirt so the folks I work with might realise that what lies beneath is a beautiful tapestry of experiences, depicting the courageous tales of their spirit's sojourns. Throughout this book, this laundress becomes seamstress, weaving together the threads of many lifetimes with a desire to create a new understanding of existence and what it means to *really* live. With this new awareness, we may transcend the urgency to forgive and seek forgiveness, realising that **absolutely nothing** happens without cause or reason, therefore, there's nothing and no one to forgive. This spiritual law is iron-clad, unwavering and absolute at all times...not just when it feels good.

Just as the sturdiest bit of cloth can tear, our lives can be ripped asunder at times, but with the needle of growth and thread of evolution, we can piece ourselves back together, fortifying and strengthening the idea that in the end, nothing or no one can harm who we *really* are. The body is merely our earthly attire, and what good are clothes if they hang in the wardrobe, wrapped in plastic, untouched and never used? Garments are meant to be worn; worked and played in. While they might become old, thread bare or out of style, rest assured there is always another set of glad rags just waiting for your soul's next adventure; *understanding this, can become your personal healing.* You simply would not believe the number of people who still actually think that they are humans seeking a spiritual connection as opposed to Divine and loving spirits relishing in the sensory infused, corporeal exploration of what it means to be human.

Allow yourself to try on these 'new threads' for size. After reading these personal accounts, you might just realise how incredibly fascinating your own threads have been so far. Some of these anecdotes may be too large, other's you may have outgrown, some you might not wear in a million years, but I'm willing to bet, somewhere in these vestments, you might just find a perfect fit...*your thread that runs so true.*

With a heart full of love and a closet full of well-worn lives, I Am...

Mary Helen

PART 1

Reflections of the Past

> *"We are attracted to another person at a soul level not because that person is our unique compliment, but because by being with that individual, we are somehow provided with an impetus to become whole ourselves."*

> *-Edgar Cayce*

And so it begins...Again

Some years ago, I had just returned home from a mini-writing retreat, where I was attempting to complete the second book in a trilogy that would eventually become known as "Promised By Heaven". I bumped in to a friend in town, soon after. She was curious about how I had gotten on during my getaway to Dublin.

"Brilliant! I had a lovely time all on my own with three nights of unbroken sleep, plus I got a good few chapters hammered out in the new book!" I quipped, with gusto. As a solo Mom, finding a few days away from my two, small girls and full-time Chiropractic and Metaphysical Healing practice was like stealing thunder from Heaven.

"Do you mind if I ask a question about the book?" My friend was eager in the asking.

"Fire away! What would you like to know?" I loved nothing more than to talk about the mystical subject matter I was presently addressing in book two of the trilogy.

My friend proceeded to ask if I intended to cover the topic of past lives, and whether or not they played a major influence on the lives we currently live. A decent question, to which I heartily answered,

"Naahh, in my experience, past lives rarely play a significant role in our lives today. They can create tendencies in some people, but it's like *this much* out of *this much*."(I was actually making a gesture comparing an inch to a mile). I had even been known to use the tidy little catch phrase, "People have so much to deal with in their current lives, why in the world would they need to look back?" Incredulous....

One would think after a lifetime of dealing with ethereal beings, near-death experiences, paranormal activity, not to mention a few past-life memories of my own, that I would have learned a little something about the way things work between *the other side* and me. If I am so presumptuous as to make a statement that is non-inclusive of *any* possibility, the powers that be are going to make a monkey out of me, each and every time. Well, toss me a banana y'all. With my hand on my heart, not gradually, but instantaneously, *every single healing session* that took place following my innocuous little statement about 'past lives' only affecting a small portion of folks, involved someone with a very serious problem in *this* lifetime, because of something that had occurred or was occurring in a *previous/parallel* existence. Me and my big mouth! For months on end... how would my teenage daughters say it? Oh yes...

I got served.

'Past lives' have gotten a bad rap, really. Those who have forgotten, sometimes make light of the concept, usually by saying something like this...

"Why was everyone a famous person like Cleopatra or Napoleon?"

Why does nearly everyone who asks that question always say the exact same thing? It's *always* Cleopatra and somebody! What they are doing is generalising the assumption that any idiot who believes in reincarnation or parallel existences, always claims to be or have been someone famous. I can now say from years of experience, this is rarely the case. Of course, there have been plenty of souls who have left a mark in the history books, but more often than not, if an individual did happen to be in any way associated with someone famous, they most likely still passed relatively unnoticed through the annals of history. Usually the period in time will identify itself with the mention of historical figures or monumental moments of bygone days that will allow me or the person I am working with to place a 'time stamp' on the lifetime during a session. ***Most of the time*** I refrain from reminding people that as fractals of the same whole, we are all technically part of every life experience that has ever been played out on the Earth plane. I tend to hold back on discussing the notion that we have the capability of accessing the collective experiences, the World Wide Web of information of everything that has ever unfolded here, with a simple shift in our vibrational state. That pill is just too big for most to swallow… It's far easier to connect with a past life or thread of lives that is specifically relevant to the client on the table that they can claim as 'their own'. We humans are funny like that.

Not all 'past life' experiences are pleasant, and not all are terribly tragic. Just think of your own life now. I'm sure you've had your ups and downs, dramas and joys, made excellent choices and some you wish you could permanently erase. There's no such thing as a 'good or bad' lifetime. When a story from 'the past' emerges in a healing session, we are always taken back to a relevant clip in the movie that will somehow assist the individual in the now they are consciously experiencing. Just think, if future you re-visited an event that current you had experienced as past you, it really wouldn't be fair to judge an entire lifetime as a success, failure, relevant or irrelevant, based on one highlights reel that turned up to shed some light on a problem area in your life. I can think of numerous decisions or circumstances in my own life that would make anyone cringe, and if any of those were to be singled out as the defining factor of my overall life challenges or contributions to date, it would paint a horribly skewed picture of who I really am.

Often times, the road to self-discovery and personal healing comes with an understanding of why certain behaviours or thought patterns can seem to dictate or interfere with day to day life. I have a dear friend who cannot explain why she becomes filled with anxiety when she sees a ship on the horizon. The sheer dread has been with her for as long as she can remember. To some, this would be no big deal, but for a woman who lives by an active shipping harbour, this can be an extremely unsettling issue to cope with, especially when she has never had a 'close call' in the water or any sort of negative incident with a ship. Another friend of mine can be minding her own business, without a care in the world until she sees any reference to Cowboys or Indians lined up on a horizon in a picture or movie. Her heart begins to race and she breaks into an angst-riddled sweat if an old western with these well-used battle scenes comes on the TV in her presence. The feeling for her is real and as you might have guessed, this city-dwelling mother of two has never personally witnessed a cavalry of soldiers or a tribe of Indians mounted on horseback in the distant skyline.

My own little girl spent the first decade of her life drilling me about the contents of every single meal I put in front of her. With no incidents having ever taken place in her short life that would have predisposed her to a fear of food, she acted as if she had been poisoned in her past, consumed by anxiety and much too concerned as to whether the food was spoiled, out of date, undercooked or containing anything to which she might have an allergic reaction. This became the focal point of *every* meal in our house throughout her early childhood until a very dear soul-mate of my own, unwittingly intervened.

My brother from another mother, Peter Bedard, came to visit from Los Angeles at the height of my daughter's fear of food. Typically the sweetest little girl, with a softness and loving nature about her, Jada immediately despised Peter when he arrived to our house. I had never seen her act this way towards anyone. Frankly, I was embarrassed and felt horrible for Peter. It was going to be a very long and miserable visit the way things were going. One evening, after days of enduring Jada's harsh comments and cutting remarks, Peter was sitting on the couch in front of the fire. Jada suddenly plopped down at his feet and began to sob. The flood gates opened wide and through her tears she spoke of betrayal and asked how Peter could have let *that* happen to her. It was a painful and a cathartic experience for both Peter and Jada. We came to realise that Jada's instant dislike towards Peter came from a cellular memory of dying (by poisonous food) and she blamed whoever Peter had been in her life at that time, for allowing it to happen to her. After she broke down and declared this revelation, she immediately softened towards Peter, genuinely mourning his departure when he left for the airport. She even gave him a gift to remember her by. (*As if there was any danger of him forgetting her or her erratic behaviour*). And the most incredible part of this story for my family? Jada immediately stopped giving me the third degree about the safety of our food. The years of strange questions, the distrust of the origins and credibility of the meals placed in front of her; it all stopped. Meeting Peter again, letting go of the hurt and feelings of betrayal from another existence allowed Jada to end an extremely stressful and damaging behaviour. Gaining insights and understanding as to the source of these bizarre circumstances can literally transform a person's life. It sure made a difference in ours.

What follows in the first section of this book are some of my favourite healing sessions in which a 'past life' or parallel biography has directly influenced an individual's present life biology. I have tried to include a wide variety of examples to show how often a hidden trigger, such as reaching a certain age, meeting a particular person or visiting a specific location can dredge up deep-seated cellular memories from another life, causing serious interference in a human's physical or emotional well-being. People are often curious as to how they will react when they start having visions of a previous or simultaneous incarnation during a session with me. "What if I get scared or feel unsafe? I'm not sure I really want to see or re-experience a past trauma for a second time!"

That's not quite the way it works for me. There are masters at the art of hypnosis and regression; psychiatrist, hypnotherapist and author, Dr Brian Weiss, probably being the most well-renowned and respected in the field of past life regression. This method, through the use of vocal cues and regression, takes a person safely into a space where they may be able to access their own impressions of past or concurrent lives. As there are many roads to one destination, there are also many roads to uncovering useful bits of data from a patient's cellular storehouse of other lives.

For me, it comes in the form of a mind movie. I will sit at

an individual's head and a virtual movie of other lifetimes, with names, dates, locations and relevant information will play out in my mind's eye. Inevitably when the information is revealed, there will be an 'aha' moment of synchronicities in this lifetime without the person having any residual traumatic feelings from the session. It's simply the way I am able to use my gifts to tap into a cellular database. There is no right or wrong way...only different ways. This was the way the gift was given to me and so far...so good.

Not all healing sessions entail a visit to another lifetime. There are many people who actually find themselves up to their eyes in current affairs, seeking healing for issues that have no tie to other lives and are based solely in the Now. The second portion of this book is dedicated to a selection of the numerous healings and encounters that I have been so fortunate to facilitate and experience, ranging from ridding bodies of cancer and other formidable maladies, to electronic voice phenomenon, to interactions with E.T.'s and ghostly apparitions. These incredible tales of the human spirit include a few of my own personal experiences and some of my favourite, mystical collaborations with friends and patients. While the 'past life' stories can be mesmerizing and utterly mind-boggling, I find present-time interactions, and their causes and cures, equally as enthralling.

In these sessions, I am able to put to good use the unusual abilities I have had since birth, which were exceptionally enhanced following my near-death experience in 1991. It all began with dreams, visions and communication with my deceased grandfather, Dr. Garland Clark. Following my high-speed collision at the age of twenty-one, I developed the ability to touch an individual and download relevant information to their life experience in order to assist them in the healing process. As the years progressed, touching even became unnecessary and distance, a non-factor.

Communication with those in spirit often includes a visual and auditory experience for me, as well. Scanning a body energetically with my eyes and physically with my hands allows me to see into a person's physiology so that I might provide them with answers about their physical and emotional state-of-being.

Conducting energy, life force or Chi through my hands allows me to alter and raise the vibratory state of another person's physical and energetic form. I hear voices…not in a schizophrenic or emotionally disturbed kind of way, but the voices of Guides belonging to a *Counsel of Beings* from whom I have been receiving incredibly accurate and insightful information for many years. And yes, I'm fully aware that it sounds weird, especially if it hasn't been something you've ever experienced in your own reality. But do remember, there are a whole lot of people out there who have. I'm one of them, and there are so many more like me who have been afraid of the ridicule, persecution and often death endured by generations of really good folks who could simply see the world a little differently. It is on their behalf that I share these stories with an open and fearless heart.

Quite possibly the most useful gift bestowed upon me at the time of my death experience is a complete disregard for what anyone thinks about me or what I do. Just imagine if I let other people's opinions stand in the way of making life a little bit easier, more fulfilling or a greater adventure for someone else. I can't even think of it! In short, I just know stuff…and knowing stuff that might connect dots that were otherwise missed medically, in counselling or through personal attempts to heal, helps me to help others help themselves.

I think it's fair to say that I have established my feelings on what a past life actually entails. Yes, I believe that a soul can reincarnate into different bodies, fitting a more linear definition of a historical measurement of time, but I have also equally witnessed fragments of our immeasurable selves that can simultaneously create in concurrent lifetimes on other planes of existence. In the first instance, a cellular *memory* may be appropriate to describe how these lives can affect us in current time. Subsequently, for those experiences that are occurring at the same time in a parallel reality, accessing an inter-connected cellular 'databank' may most adequately describe how I gather information. For ease of flow in reading, when I make reference the term 'past life' in the pages that follow, I am referring to one of these two scenarios.

Open your heart and your mind and truly immerse yourself in the experiences you are about to read. Grab yourself a cup of tea, sit back and allow these true life characters to bring their wisdom to you. It might be more than a cup of tea you'll need by the end of this book!

Phantoms of the Past

Every now and again, a tale unfolds that causes the hair on the back of my neck to stand on end. Our case-studies begin with a blood-chilling example of why sometimes it's not so pleasant to have interacted with someone famous or *infamous* in the past. When Eleanor had inquired about a healing session for her daughter, I had no idea that she was to be the first in a very long list of past-life regressions to cross my threshold. Because of one little nonchalant remark as I described previously about the insignificance of these lifetimes in some people's present day issues; the Multiverse had decided to teach me a valuable lesson about passing judgement concerning topics that I really knew very little about.

Eleanor spoke with genuine concern as she filled me in on a bit of her daughter's history. She described her daughter, Fran's, life as nice and *normal* up until two years prior to our conversation. She was married, very much in love with, and deeply loved by her husband, had several beautiful young children, and was an active part of her community. When she wasn't travelling to and from Wales to visit her husband's family, she was always on the go at home. It did not take long before Fran, or the ones who loved her, noticed the disturbing changes in her behaviour. At first, there were small peculiarities, like Fran needing to stay in the car rather than getting out, when picking up the children from school.

The fear was gradually building as she began to leave the car parked at the front door of a shop where she could see it all times, in case she needed to make a quick escape. When she first sent her husband and children to visit his family in Wales without her, because she was too nervous to travel, everyone got concerned.

Eventually, Fran's fears got the best of her and she became a prisoner of her own home.

The only way Fran made it in to see me one bleak and dreary winter afternoon, was by surrounding herself with a small entourage of family members who encircled her and walked her from the car to the door of my office. She was shaking like a leaf as she made them swear that they would wait outside in the car, in case she needed to make a break for it. We were close in age, both mothers. My heart went out to her as I tried to fathom the depths of her despair. This beautiful looking woman laughed anxiously, as she expressed her doubt as to how a simple session with me could make any impact on her debilitating phobia. Her doctors were at a complete loss and had eventually diagnosed her with severe depression. Fran filled me in on the crippling fear that had taken control of every waking moment of her life, the fear that had imprisoned her in her home for the last two years. She didn't know how or why it had started. I told her she had nothing to lose. She agreed, as she got up onto the plinth. I held on to her ankles, closed my eyes and let her body fill me in on the details of the untold story.

Within moments, a dark tale began to unfold, not of Fran's past as Fran, but of the life of another woman in late, 19th century London. My mind began to race as I heard the name Martha repeated over and over again. I tried to quiet the noise in my head and searched for a surname and physical description. I was overtaken by the smell of alcohol and body odour. I felt sick to my stomach as I realised that this woman made a regular practice of selling herself to earn a few shillings. The next visual caused me to gasp out loud. There, at the bottom of a dark, dank stairwell was a short, heavy set woman, her skirts pulled up over her waist, with multiple stab wounds covering her lifeless body.

"This is Martha. Martha Tabram."

The voices in my head spoke with precision.

"This is a cellular memory. In the last few years leading up to the age of 39, Fran's body, her energy incarnate, has developed a morbid fear of being harmed

again in such a way that would result in her death in this lifetime, at or around the same age as her most recent embodiment as Martha Tabram. These emotions are unfounded in this incarnation; however, the feeling is strong, so deeply embedded in her soul's memory, that she has become paralysed by this experience. Your role is to connect the two, integrating the past while releasing her in the present."

That stupid little remark I had so flippantly made about past lives and present issues had seriously come back to haunt me. How in the world was I going to explain this revelation to the already petrified lady, now uncharacteristically calm on the table in front of me? All I could do was gently share the truth.

Much to my surprise, Fran handled the insight remarkably well. It was as if she finally had something she could work with. The doctor's suggestions of phobia due to depression or anxiety had never resonated with her, and as gruesome as the circumstances were, this explanation seemed to make sense. When our time had come to a close, Fran got off the table, looking lighter, certainly less fearful and she was actually laughing. She picked up her shoes and carried them out into the waiting room. The office was vacant. Dusk had set in, and the sky was overcast and dull outside of my large, shop-front window. As Fran tied her shoe-laces, she looked at me and said,

"You know, that story really doesn't frighten me at all, even though I feel sad for that woman...for me, you say." She chuckled at the idea that she might have actually been 'the other woman'.

"All that keeps coming into my mind now is "Jack the Ripper".

I felt that familiar gnawing in the pit of my stomach. *Why had she just said that?*

I turned the key in the door, ready to wave out to the car where her family was anxiously waiting. Before I could make a move, Fran gave me a big hug, thanked me, and walked out the door, down the sidewalk and into the car *on her own*. She didn't even realise what she was doing.

Her bewildered mother gave me a thumb's up at the sight of her daughter casually strolling out the door unaccompanied. In total shock, they stared at me, mouths agape, as they drove away. I made a mad dash for the computer and Googled the name Martha Tabram. After what I discovered, it was *me* who was in need of an escort out of the office, as I now officially had the creeps.

Thank heavens for Wikipedia. Five minutes after this woman had made the prophetic statement about "Jack the Ripper"; I was looking at an eerie post-mortem photograph, reading a detailed story of one *Martha Tabram*. Born in Southwark, *London* in 1849, Martha White had married Samuel Tabram, a foreman in a furniture warehouse, in 1869. They had two sons in 1871 and '72, just three years prior to their breakup, due to her chronic issues with drinking. (*Remember the strong smell of alcohol during the session*). From 1876 to July of 1888, she had lived on and off with Henry Turner, a carpenter in Whitechapel. It was during this time that she had taken to *prostitution* to supplement her income earned by selling trinkets on the streets.

In August of 1888, **Martha Tabram** had been out drinking with another 'lady of the night' and two soldiers, in the "Angel and Crown" public house. When the women parted ways with their clients just before midnight, Martha Tabram went to George Yard, a small alley between Wentworth and Whitechapel High Street. At 2 am there had been cries of *"Murder!"* in the street outside of the tenements adjacent to the alleyway. Violence and shouting weren't uncommon in this area so it wasn't until around 5 am that a dock labourer on his way to work discovered Martha Tabram's dead body *at the bottom of a stairwell. Covered in multiple stab wounds, her skirts were* above *her waist, her body lying in a sexual position.*

There were investigations and numerous inquiries, particularly of soldiers from the Tower of London, but no suspect was ever charged with her murder.

What makes this all so fascinating? Only a few weeks after her murder, there were five highly publicised deaths that became known as the "canonical five"; the victims of "Jack the Ripper".

Although it has never been officially connected, there has apparently been much speculation that the murder of Martha Tabram, a prostitute in the now renowned Whitechapel district, may have actually been the first victim of the world's most famous serial killer.

By connecting the dots for Fran, she was able to release an incapacitating phobia of fearing for her safety in public places; one that had simply been triggered by approaching the same age that her 'other' self had been when she was so brutally murdered. Fran's husband got his wife back, her children had their very energetic mommy again, and her own mother could now take her out of the house for a cup of coffee. Fran has since started travelling to her in-laws again, in Wales. She shops, collects her children at the school gate and has now reclaimed her life from the clutches of a horrid memory she didn't consciously know existed. Why lose a life twice at the hands of a man who now only lives in infamy?

REFLECTIONS

The floodgates opened with the reality-altering revelation of Martha Tabram; the stories becoming more bizarre with each passing session. Although I was totally stupefied, this marked the beginning of a time that has been absolutely enthralling for me. The pain and heartache that so many of my clients have endured while dragging the ball and chain of a devastating past life experience, has been all too real for them. I have been asked if it simply isn't the power of suggestion that makes these people whole again. My answer to that a decade ago…"I really don't know". My answer today…" I really don't care".

If the scenarios that present themselves as intricately detailed 'mind movies' of another life are merely a fantastic creation of my brain or the patient's brain or some combination of our collective consciousness - so be it. If these are, in fact, images of lifetimes already lived or simultaneously being played out on another plane of existence-that's fine, too. The truth of it is somehow, someway, the release of these past or concurrent life cellular memories is allowing people to miraculously accomplish lasting healing in present time…and that's good enough for me.

Baby Steps

This next series of events totally knocked me for a loop. From a doctor/patient perspective, it was exhilarating. As a mother, it tore my heart in two. I marvelled at the impact that a previous incarnation and her soul's recovery plan had on the current life of my new friend, Sue.

A bundle of nerves when she walked through the door of the reception room, Sue was desperate for help. The last couple of years of her life had been a relentless nightmare. Sue had been happily married, a well-adjusted mother of two, physically fit and mentally engaged with her family, both socially and in the home. That was, until a few months after she had given birth to her third child. She looked pale, the dark circles under her eyes were a testament to the fact that she hadn't slept properly in a very long time and her breath was shallow. I knew that when she had been in the full of her health, she was striking in appearance. I could still see that beautiful woman, despite the toll that her ordeal had taken on her physically. With an eerie calm, like one found in the eye of a hurricane, Sue shared a story that left me utterly speechless.

When she had given birth to Sophie, they had initially bonded as any mother would hope to with her new-born baby. According to Sue, it was a gradual process, over a couple of months, when the *feelings* started to pop into her head. There was an inexplicable and overwhelming sensation that caused Sue to feel afraid and unsafe when she was around little Sophie. On the first Halloween night after Sophie's birth, Sue had her first 'breathing attack'. When she simply could not catch her breath, the panic ensued and filled her with terror. Sophie's intensity had become too much. *Intensity?* She was only a few months old.

In the days, weeks and months that followed, Sue did everything to avoid being near her baby when at all possible. When Sophie would wake and remain awake, every night after being put to bed; Sue described these as her darkest times. In the night, the horrible blackness, with just Sue, the baby, and her confusing thoughts, an awful, sinking feeling left her too afraid to go to sleep, terrified that this infant was actually going to harm her in some way. She knew it seemed crazy, but the sensation was just so real. She felt boxed off by other people and their unhelpful suggestions that she may be experiencing the 'baby blues', postpartum depression or some form of a nervous breakdown. Her family and friends understandably could not grasp the idea that Sue was unable to embrace this darling little girl with the captivating eyes.

The January after Sophie's birth was when Sue finally felt that she could no longer go on. She felt totally on her own, with nobody to help her, despite her husband's constant presence. He had no idea what was happening to his wife, no inkling of the gravity that Sue was unable to handle the pressure any longer. She genuinely thought she was going mad. She was losing weight; sleep deprived; now battling thoughts of ending her own life. She told me that she only existed for her husband, Paul, and her two other daughters. She couldn't even force herself to go to the gym, which had previously been a great passion and place of respite, because she was so lost in her thoughts of helplessness. Eventually, she checked herself into St. John of God's Psychiatric Hospital. She was smothered, feeling as if her baby was in control of her life, so much so, that she even attempted to have Health Services look in to having the baby fostered. Her husband was dumbfounded by this idea, and opposed it vehemently. Sue was convinced that Sophie had a glint in her eye, that she *knew* what she was doing to her mother, not acting sinisterly around anyone else.

What we discovered, was that while the baby Sophie may not have been consciously aware of what she was doing, there was a scenario playing out that was like nothing I had ever witnessed. I sat behind Sue's head, closed my eyes and waited for the voices and 'the movie'.

It didn't take long before I saw the disconsolate woman in my mind. Not Sue, but an incarnation of her vacant-eyed soul in another time. Married off to a man that she did not love, he took her far away from her family and kept her prisoner, as his wife, with his overzealous 'love'. This man was cruel to her, justifying his terrible acts of abuse because he loved her so much. He never allowed contact with her family, leaving her isolated and alone in the home she wasn't allowed to leave, awaiting his next act of violence. There was one person, a policeman in the village, who knew of this severe domestic situation. He was an acquaintance of the husband, yet his own fear of this man's irrational behaviour meant that he never spoke up or intervened. With absolutely no hope of a future that didn't involve pain, terror and desperation, the disparaged young woman eventually took her own life.

This despondent, shell of a mortal, was Sue. The policeman who wanted to help, but was too paralysed by his own fear, was now her current husband. The horribly abusive man who had alienated his helpless wife from the rest of the world? The baby, Sophie.

Straightaway, Sue's feelings, her fears, her inability to get close to her own child, all began to make sense. Because the woman in the previous incarnation had ended her life not by a soul plan suicide, but one that was the result of overwhelming anguish, these same members of Sue's soul group had incarnated together to allow Sue to face the feelings in an altered setting; the utter despair and the urge to escape misery by her own hand, under a different set of circumstances. They had provided her with the opportunity to choose life this time, (or death again). Sue's mouth was open, her eyes were wide, but something in her had shifted. There was a sudden realisation that she hadn't gone mad, that she hadn't created these feelings out of her inability to cope with a third child. There was actually a reason…a plan of their own design.

In the sessions to follow, Sue brought Sophie along. The healing that took place between them was nothing short of extraordinary. You could have knocked us over with a feather the first time Sue brought her bubbly little tot with the silky dark hair and big, bright eyes to her appointment. The child toddled over to my tuning forks, just 'happened' to pick up 528 hertz, the mother of all frequencies, resonating with human DNA and referred to as 'the miracle frequency', and started striking it with the mallet and waving it over her mother. Gobsmacked, Sue and I looked at each other, looked back at the child, then we laughed until literally, we cried; tears of joy, tears of relief, tears of awe, really. I was able to telepathically communicate to Sophie, not yet two years old, that the mission was accomplished.

Sue reported that following our discovery, Sophie's behaviour immediately changed. Sue's husband, Paul, also became involved. This had been a difficult time for him, as well, and he was open-minded and accepting of the fact that something out of the ordinary had deeply affected his family.

Sue carefully began to rebuild her life. She overcame her darkest days, learning patience and tolerance not only with Sophie, but with herself. She retrained her thought processes and the habitual patterns of how she deals with and reacts to stress. The panic attacks, the breathing difficulties have all subsided. Sue has become a student of her own lives. For me, she has become a most inspirational teacher, as I continue to work with those who have issues in their tissues, from some other reality.

REFLECTIONS

I am eternally grateful that I was given the chance to witness a life-changing healing in this family. I am equally indebted to them for their courage to share this incredibly difficult time, so that others might benefit. Only recently, nearly ten years later, Sue described the light and joy that her deep bond with Sophie, a vibrant and deeply loving child, brings to her life. For me, this story is a very good reminder that we never know what people are going through behind closed doors. It also gives us great insight into the real meaning of karma. So often, karma is described as some kind of punishment or cosmic retribution when in actuality, the repetition of lessons with members of our soul group through multiple incarnations, points more to the idea that karma is the conscious creation of our soul's desire to work through a human life lesson from every possible angle.

Perfect Murder

Have you ever met someone who is perfectly beautiful, yet has absolutely no idea just how magnificent they really are? Enter Jacinta; unassuming and shy, yet quietly powerful. When I asked Jacinta my standard introductory question of why she was really on my table at this time in her life, her answer was short and precise. *Trust.* She had managed to make it in to the autumn of her life, taking care of herself, of her own needs, interacting with the world, trusting *no one.* She had come to me because she wanted to know why. Her list of physical challenges was peculiar, to say the least; an intermittent numbness on the left side of the body, palpitations, stabbing pains and eye and ear sensitivities, none which turned up with a plausible explanation from the experts.

Although her ailments really made no sense medically, somehow Jacinta inherently knew that metaphysically, these symptoms stemmed from somewhere, sometime other than now.

During hard times in Ireland many years ago, it was not uncommon for one or more children to be 'farmed' out to the extended family. As a child, Jacinta had been sent from her home in the country to live with an aunt and uncle in the 'big smoke' of Dublin. She recalls that she loved and respected these relatives, but she was always frightened of the way in which they resolved conflict in the home.

"I have vivid memories of my aunty waving a butcher's knife in the heat of an argument, and this absolutely terrified me as a child!"

Still, Jacinta intuitively knew that her issues of trust for her safety and well-being had occurred long before these episodes of violent 'conflict resolution' from her childhood. Jacinta also admitted to having a bizarre, secret fascination starting at around the age of eleven, with crime stories, murder and the macabre; totally uncharacteristic of her exceedingly mild-mannered demeanour. Over a series of sessions, her *real* story began to unfold.

The stench of sweat, the palpable fear in the air of religious domination, surrounded a casual, yet confidential conversation between two men in England, in the year 1457. While sipping a hot drink in a public house, one friend innocently shared with the other, that he thought it very strange that all of the artistic imagery currently portraying the likenesses of Christ and the Virgin Mary were Anglo-Saxon in appearance. Wouldn't they have been Middle Eastern in ethnicity?

In the next scene of my mind movie, this same man was walking through a small alleyway, where a brief skirmish ensued and a dagger was fatally thrust through his gut. Betrayed by fear, this man's 'friend' had reported him a heretic, and his innocent curiosity had sentenced him to an early, unjust death.

Several centuries passed between scenes, as Jacinta and I simultaneously witnessed in our minds, a man committing murder out of pure malice. The exact date and location were not shown, yet the feeling, the brute force and anger of the murderer was palpable. I jotted down the information that was coming to me as Jacinta was silently reliving the story in her own mind; we were unaware, however, that the tales which were independently revealing themselves were *identical* until we spoke at the end of her session. This was truly interesting, as Jacinta seemed to be watching the same mind movie as me, which in my case, was quite untypical.

Another hundred years would pass, as a new scene played out of a desperate man and his destitute family. They were all starving, weak with fear and hunger and living in squalor on the streets of France. The otherwise unobtrusive family man had been forced to murder an attacker, in order to save his own household. The last of his dignity was lost to this necessary act of violence.

While I sat stunned, Jacinta, in all of her wisdom, clearly resonated with each of these men. The details of the stories had not seemed to be important, but the feelings, the *frequency* of the anger, the fear, and the desperation were the key. Betrayed then murdered, madman turned murderer, then murderer to be saviour of an innocent family. Her realisations of the past in connection to her present struggles had brought her to a new understanding of herself.

"I've stopped looking outside of myself for validation. I trust myself, who I am today, and now seek guidance through my own healing." Jacinta later mused. She now understood that a soul will seek to know a subject so intimately, that it is willing to play all parts, from noble to corrupt, in order to acquire a deeper understanding of life.

Her symptoms, each correlating to injuries sustained by the murdered and murderers of her other lives, have abated, her inability to trust others is now benign, and this amazing woman has embarked on a path of self-discovery that may just see her choose to love and be loved, but most important, to trust and love herself.

REFLECTIONS

The sessions that took place during this time have altered the way that I listen, share information, or pass judgement on the cause or cure of people's suffering. I also began to reflect on my own lifetimes and how these experiences have contributed to the strengths and weaknesses of my character and physical form today. Why would anyone want to look at their past or concurrent lives when they have so much to deal with this time around? I humbly hold up my hand and say, "I couldn't have been more mistaken."

Does it happen every time? No. There are equally as many people who are wading through the muck of the issues created in this life. I have learned to never ever say never, when it comes to discovering the original source of someone's pain, be it physical or emotional. Understanding these concepts has been vital to the way I have been able to assist others in their healing.

Out of the Mouths of Babes

When I was still practising chiropractic, I had a patient who would come in for her monthly maintenance adjustments and tell me the most horrific tales of what she and her husband were enduring in their fervent quest to become parents. Linda had severe endometriosis and polycystic ovaries, which had made getting pregnant an absolute nightmare. Following painful surgery, which included drilling into the ovaries, as well as subsequent hormone treatments, she had eventually managed to bypass her body's inexplicable resistance to motherhood. This sweet, raven-haired angel would finally realise her dream of having a baby.

I cared for Linda throughout the pregnancy, making sure that her spine was in alignment and that her nervous system was free of interference so that she could sustain the growing foetus she and her husband had fought so tenaciously to create. Her son was eventually born, but not without serious hardship. An emergency caesarean and a life-threatening reaction to medication during the birth had caused Linda to nearly choke to death on the operating table. Once she was out of the woods and finally held her beautiful boy, she put the horror behind her... *or so she thought.*

Linda's longing to give her son a sibling overtook the memories of nearly losing her own life during his entry into the world. For three years, she and her husband attempted to get pregnant again, to no avail. After being told by her doctor that things didn't look good and that the waiting list to see a consultant was at least ten months long, Linda was in total despair. Her husband was due to be deployed by the Irish Army in a few months and her chances of getting pregnant in that time, after three years of constant trying, were slim to none.

I had taken an indefinite hiatus from chiropractic due to an injury in 2012, and my practice as a metaphysical healer was now my primary focus. I was hosting workshops and public speaking in addition to working on the third book in the "Promised By Heaven" trilogy. My dear friend and fellow author, Peter Bedard, had come to Ireland from Los Angeles to present a workshop on self-healing techniques he has developed and written about in his book, "Convergence Healing". (It was on this same visit that my daughter's phobia of contaminated food, mentioned earlier, was healed when she eight)

I was delighted to see my former patient, Linda, as a participant in the workshop. After Peter had finished his presentation, I got the chance to catch up with Linda, as I hadn't seen much of her since I was no longer in practice. She shared with me her difficult story of the past few years; the numerous failed attempts to have another baby. She had signed up for Peter's seminar to learn some new tools to assist her with the emotional links to her physical inability to conceive. *She would be putting these new skills to use much sooner than she thought.*

My heart went out to her because if ever there was a natural at being a loving and compassionate mommy, it was Linda. She said that she knew in her heart that 'something wasn't right'. Yes, there were the issues with her polycystic ovaries and endometriosis, but she had a gnawing, gut feeling that *something else* was blocking her from becoming pregnant.

With absolutely no clue as to what she was getting herself into, Linda booked in with me for a healing session, hoping that maybe the block was from the fear created when she nearly choked to death on the delivery table, three years earlier. To be honest, that's what I, too, expected to uncover. When I knew she was coming, I was prepared to walk her through that frightening experience, shake hands with the horrendous memories and put it to rest. *What was revealed on that day was something neither of us had anticipated.*

As is customary when I facilitate a session, I placed my hands on Linda's head and asked the Divine to show me how I could best assist her in healing. Almost immediately, a story began to unfold with such speed, that I had to scramble to get paper and pen as I was flooded with imagery, names, dates and locations. The virtual movie played out in my mind's eye. My heart was pounding because the first impression I received was that of an older lady being publicly hanged as punishment for unspeakable crimes involving the murders of numerous young children. I looked at Linda's sweet face, eyes closed; calm and trusting. I felt ill.

"Dear God!" I thought to myself. "Please tell me that her fertility issues aren't tied to a former life in which she was responsible for these deaths." My stomach churned at the thoughts of telling this dear soul about the horror story unfolding in front of me. Yet, I knew from years of experience, we aren't always the heroes of our own stories. We play *every* role as lifetimes present the opportunity to learn and grow through multiple perspectives... heroic, archaic, indifferent or in service to the *dark* or *light*.

The words were nearly writing themselves, they came with such determination, as if finally they had been freed from the secret confines of Linda's subconscious.

Amelia Dyer 1896 (hanging), Evelina Marman-Barmaid, pregnant by customer, boarding house, baby Doris, Cheltenham, ad in paper, adoption £10 (temporary), baby's neck wrapped in dressing tape, slow suffocation, same tape used on another baby, dumped in river, second to last victim, multiple deaths, life broken after child's death, if only killer had been caught a few days before physical/emotional block=fear of death around childbirth

Almost immediately, my concerns were quelled as the rest of this unthinkable tale unravelled. I frantically scribbled down the sordid details with such speed, that Linda even commented about the sound of my pen scratching across the paper.

"Jaysus, it must be awful!" Her Irish brogue attempted to bring a little levity to the moment. Little did she know...

Police photo of Amelia Dyer after being arrested in 1896 Courtesy of Wikipedia

When the influx of information finally stopped, I asked Linda to sit up. Always smiling, she knew that the look on my face was one of shock and the deepest empathy. I began to tell her the bizarre tale of her life as a bar-maid, Evelina Marman, and the most unfortunate circumstances surrounding the death of her baby girl at the hands of a con-artist and murderer by the name of Amelia Dyer. She was more intrigued than freaked out, thank heavens. Both of us were immediately curious as to whether or not there was any record of this event online. I literally ran out to the front desk of the office to get my iPad, heart pounding as I returned to find Linda ever so calm but with the strangest look on her face. It was like she knew it was over. I began to plug in the names and dates that had so readily handed themselves over during the session, right there in front of Linda. As the story goes, we were both rendered speechless.

There it was in black and white; a detailed account of the murderess I had seen in my mind's eye. My skin crawled as we read her story; names and dates matching those I had scratched into my notebook with one hand, as I had touched Linda's head with the other. This woman was real. Neither of us had ever heard of her, but her existence in 1896 was now irrefutably significant to the story of Linda's life in the twenty-first century.

Linda stared at the picture of Amelia Dyer and was overcome with a sense of sadness and strangely, a *knowing*. "Well, darlin', it looks like we found our why. Now let's see if we can clear this thing", I said, having her lie down again. I asked her to focus on the fact that the cellular memories of her life as Evelina Marman, the mother of a murdered child, were no longer serving her. I encouraged her to express her gratitude and compassion for the terrible hardships this woman had endured. Tears began to form as she connected with this deeply disturbing memory. The auric field of light energy around her body began to pulsate as she told herself that this lifetime as Linda was so different. She was safe, loving and deeply loved, wanting nothing more than to share her fortunate circumstances with another child.

"After my session with Mary Helen, all of these feelings made sense and everything sat comfortably with me, even though it was terribly sad. I processed and grieved for what my soul had endured and for the first time ever, gave myself and my body the comfort and love that it deserved. I talked to my body and asked what it needed to heal. The word heat would pop into my head, so I would place a lavender heat pack on my stomach. I remember saying to my husband, "I am going to heal my body".

I talked to my body as I would talk to a dear friend who had been through a traumatic experience. I finally understood why I obsessed about having my son next to me at all times. It was the overwhelming fear of losing him, although I never knew from where or when this fear had come.
Four weeks after my session, I was sitting on my bed playing with my three year old son. "Mammy, you won't believe it! There's a tiny little baby in your tummy!" My heart sank with disappointment as it would have been an absolute miracle if it were true. "And Mammy", he smiled, as his angelic little face gleamed with certainty. "It's a baby girl."
I told my husband, who nervously smiled, as not to disappoint me. "Don't even be thinking of it. You'll only get your hopes up and we've been here so many times before." He was right, but part of me hoped beyond hope that my little boy, (who often spoke to strangers about their loved ones in Heaven), was the one who was right this time.

Two weeks passed and I couldn't stand it any longer. I did a pregnancy test without telling anyone. I will never forget that moment. I looked at the panel on the stick with one eye squinted because I knew it would be negative. I screamed out loud as before me, was a big, strong, definite positive. I simply could not believe it! I rang my hubbie, screaming and crying! When he eventually realised that I wasn't being attacked or murdered, I delivered the news. He instructed me to go straight to the doctor, because deep down, he actually thought the test was faulty and he couldn't bare the disappointment again. On September 9th, 2014, I sent Mary Helen the following text:

Hi Mary Helen
Hope all is fabulous with you. I just wanted to thank you again for the healing session and fill you in on the news. After our session, I was determined to heal myself. I actually can't believe I am writing this, but we found out this morning that I am six weeks pregnant! Last thing you said to me after my session just over six weeks ago was that ANYTHING is possible! Well, I'm proof in the pudding! We are over the moon! As soon as you showed me everything from my past life, it all just sat right. I finally felt content and was able to put a lot to rest. I'm on top of the world

Eight months later, a beautiful baby girl arrived. I wondered if she was hesitant to come back in to this world because towards the end of labour, her little heart stopped beating-she had temporarily suffocated in the womb. But, thanking all forces and all angels, she came back to us to share this wonderful journey. When I eventually saw her for the first time following the distressing birth, I said, "Welcome back, little angel." I knew I was looking into the eyes of the baby I had loved before. Little Doris and I were reunited again."

–Linda

REFLECTIONS

During our session together, I had been invited into Linda's lifetime as Evelina Marmon by her higher self, her great I AM, long enough to witness her soul's plan and how this complex memory had temporarily thwarted her attempts to conceive another child. I visibly witnessed her energetic patterns change when her biography was revealed within her biology. Never have I felt such privilege to be invited in to a soul's journey, simply to stitch two lives together, so this beautiful woman could create the healing necessary to fulfil her soul's plan as Linda.

The Second Time Around

Nearly two years following this incredible interaction with Linda, who, by the way, has now given birth to her third child, the oddest thing occurred. Many healing sessions later, a lovely lady came in to my office and stretched out on my table, smiled and chirped, "You tell me what's going on. I'm saying nothing."

This can be a bit distressing when someone says this to me, not because I think they are out to trip me up or catch me out, but because they might have the impression that I'm a fortune teller of sorts. Don't get me wrong, fortune tellers have their place along the path to self-discovery for many people. They are actually quite popular here, in Ireland. All who strive to contribute to a seeker of truth have some form of value. It simply depends on what leg of the journey an individual is on, as to who can most effectively deliver the type of information that will be most relevant.

Personally, I try in earnest, to steer people away from the temptation of asking about things which are not set in stone; outcomes that are dependent on their own actions, where they are and what lessons they are learning along the path of life. "Will I find love? Is my mother going to die soon? Will I have a financial windfall?" Answering these types of questions serves only to satisfy curiosity, parlour tricks as far as I'm concerned, really having nothing to do with assisting someone in discovering their own innate ability to heal the body or progress the soul's journey, however, I also accept that this is simply where some people are. At the end of the day, I believe everything serves a purpose whether we like it or not.

I take the responsibility of each seed of information that I plant very seriously. I know the impact it can make. Those who regularly have their future told, tend never to talk about the inaccurate information they have received; the twins that were never born or the pile of money up for inheritance from an uncle that didn't exist. Human nature causes folks to latch on to the things like, "Mr. Right will arrive in six months", because we really and truly want to believe in the happy endings that might just happen. I spend so much time trying to create acceptance, ultimately resulting in happiness around the intended outcomes of our soul's plan. It's just a different inning of the same ball game.

Yes, I can see things past and future, and yes, I can download information revealing the reasons behind a person's current state of affairs, but it doesn't take an intuitive gift to placate the inquisitive queries of future or fortune seekers. Usually, these personalities tend to continuously pursue psychics and mediums until eventually they are told what they want to hear, not necessarily what is their truth. There are also those who move from medium to medium, constantly attempting to connect with their dead, even after a clear message has been delivered by their loved one that they are alive and well in spirit. It's a difficult conversation to have with someone who is immovable in their grief. It's also a conversation I have had to have on numerous occasions. Sadly, these are the ones who torture themselves, hoping to never lose touch with someone who has moved on. They feel that if they don't keep contacting those in spirit, they will somehow be forgotten or worse, that they hope that the apparition of the deceased may walk with them through the remainder of their life on Earth until they meet again in Heaven. It's an unfortunate by-product of the way society at large has been taught to view death. I am trying my very best to reshape the death archetype that we have been sold in the name of religion and control. So much so, that in 2018, I co-authored a book with Patricia Scanlan, Aidan Storey and Pamela Young entitled "Bringing Death To Life"- An Uplifting Exploration of Living, Dying, the Soul Journey and the Afterlife.

Death is but a doorway, and a revolving doorway at that. An entrance and exit to be used at our will to experience life incarnate in whatever realm we choose. Religion has not only made it a scary doorway, but a single use, one way system with a door that slams shut behind it's user, permanently sealing them into an eternity of interminable bliss or everlasting hell and damnation. Seriously…

I choose to use my abilities to quell fear, build spiritual muscle and to remind people of their own divinity. Sometimes this involves bringing up events from the past that I could have known nothing about. Other times a person may simply need to hear from a deceased loved one in order to move on from their grief. Respite from ill health or emotional trauma is as unique as every sweet soul who crosses my threshold, but the one constant, is with understanding comes healing.

I digress…

Let's get back to the woman on my table who wanted to say nothing and for me to tell all. So there I was, not staring at a blank canvas, but an exquisite portrait of a beautiful lady, nearly the same age as me. I spoke with her body, tapped in to her history and as with many women who have sought my services; it was revealed that she was unable to conceive, after at least *twenty years* of trying.

"Dorothy", I enquired. "Have you been told that there is a medical cause behind your inability to get pregnant? Ok, I can feel that one ovary isn't quite up to scratch, but the other is absolutely fine. I take it your husband has also been checked? I'm just not feeling that this is physical."

She explained that they had both been through a barrage of testing and there was, in fact, no physical reason that they could not create a baby.

"I hope you have an open mind," I chuckled, because this is about to get wild!" She laughed and said that she was open to anything and that she really needed to get to the bottom of this so that she could either get pregnant or let go of the idea once and for all.

I asked if she had really and truly wanted children. She explained that the endless questions from family and friends had put an exorbitant amount of pressure on her. In truth, she wasn't really sure if she was bothered either way. She said she had often thought over the years that she and her husband weren't meant to have children. It was a *knowing*, although she didn't *know* why. At that point, the voices began. I excused myself and sat down behind Dorothy, placing my hands on her head as I listened. When the names, dates and locations started coming at me like a freight train, I grabbed pen and paper and hurriedly scratched out the words. It took a few minutes, but all of a sudden, the words on the page in front of me began to look strangely familiar, as in, I had heard this exact same story from a different angle, a long time ago.

Baby farming/ 1895(ish)/Wales/England

Martha Corbett was just 17 when she gave birth to baby Tilly Jones in a village in North Wales on Braxton Street (Court?)Her boyfriend (Jones) loved her and was prepared to take complete responsibility, eager to marry Martha and to raise their child together. Upon hearing the news that Martha was pregnant, her parents forbade her to see the father of her unborn child. She was sent to an aunt in Berkshire, U.K., where she eventually gave birth. Under strict instructions from her parents, an ad was placed in the paper for adoption. The ad was answered by a lady named Mrs. Thomas. The stodgy older woman who came for the child insisted on £12 in a lump sum payment. Martha was devastated. Once the baby was born, Martha remained in Berkshire with her aunt. Both she and Jones went on to marry other people. Jones was eventually killed while fighting in WW1. Martha begrudgingly married a widower with three children. The two girls and boy despised Martha and made life a living hell for her, behind their father's back. It had been a miserable existence.

Mrs. Thomas? That rang a bell. Upon further investigation, Mrs. Thomas had been an alias of Amelia Dyer, a name I hadn't thought of since my session with Linda, two years earlier. Could this be possible? I had just encountered a second victim of the most horrendous serial killer of children that England (and quite possibly the world) had ever known. Linda and Dorothy were not from the same towns, not even the same part of the country, but somehow, these two women who shared the same physical challenge, shared something far more horrific and had both found their way to me.

When Linda was released from her past as the mother of the baby who was Amelia Dyer's second to last murder victim, her body freed itself of the terror surrounding having children, including the expectation that pregnancy would ultimately end in death and horror. This was her soul's plan and instantly allowed her to conceive (Linda told me it happened the same night following her session!)

Dorothy, on the other hand, made a peaceful and welcome release of the idea that she *had* to be a mother this time around. She was visibly relieved as she connected to, remembered even, that she and her husband had decided to spend this lifetime enjoying the love that they never were allowed to share as Martha Corbett and Mr. Jones.

REFLECTIONS

Understanding the why is a powerful elixir, and while Linda and Dorothy had the same why, their healings manifested in very different forms. The strength and trust exhibited by these two ladies spoke to my soul, as a mother and a healer. There are so many women who have faced the challenges that both of these women endured. For some, it's the insatiable feeling that sharing the love of a child would complete the family unit. For others, the pressures of being a single woman, or a childless thirty-something couple, means constant dodging of the expectations and barrage of questions by well-meaning family and friends. As I have been told numerous times by folks who have walked in those shoes, it can be enough to drive a person insane.

Most importantly, the feelings of guilt or inadequacy can be put to rest when one finally has the answer to the seemingly unanswerable questions in life. Healing doesn't always mean getting the result we thought we were looking for. Many times it means understanding the result we need in order to get on with life. Resentment turns to forgiveness and ultimately transcends to understanding. A state of peace and resolution in the heart of someone in turmoil is equally as meaningful as any physical healing.

Heal Hitler!

I can't actually count the number of people who have come to me for sessions that end up having a tie on some level to the devastation caused by WW2 and Hitler. It's interesting to note, that whenever I am teaching a workshop or speaking at a public event, inevitably someone always asks about the most hideously charismatic politician of the twentieth century. For most people, this man represents the darkest, most despicable aspects of the human psyche. When talking about soul plans and what happens when we die, a hand always goes up and *without fail*, someone will ask the million dollar question. "So, are you asking me to believe me that Hitler went to Heaven? You actually expect me to entertain the idea that God or whoever is up there let this soul escape punishment?" The interesting thing about the question is that *I'm never talking about Hitler or anything having to do with him* when the question is asked. He just seems to be the go to guy for eternal damnation.

To a person who cannot digest the concept that not only do souls come into this world for growth and expansion, but that someone has to play the role of the 'bad guy' in order to create the experiences necessary for spiritual growth, no explanation is really possible. These are the folks who can't get their heads around why bad things happen to good people. In short, these are our friends who still believe that duality and separation from Source is something more than a tool or somehow slipped through the cracks of God's omnipotent plan.

Liz came to me with a most unusual complaint. She was a vivacious, extremely attractive woman, single, yet socially active and in the prime of her sex life. Every time Liz reached a point of physical intimacy with a partner, an incredible tension would overcome her body until her muscles became so tight, that penetration was impossible. Instinct and the seemingly obvious would automatically prompt one to ask about past sexual trauma, rape, abuse or inappropriate touching during her childhood in Belfast. *Nothing.* With her hand on her heart she swore that she had never remotely experienced anything as a child or as an adult that could be mistaken for sexual abuse. I scanned her energy field, tapped into her history, looking for signs of suppression or denial. There were none.

That unmistakeable sensation of the voices and impending visions from another time, place or space came over me. I sat with my hands on Liz's head, with dim lights and the soothing sounds of lapping ocean waves floating out of my trusty, old CD player. Suddenly, I was in Ludenscheid, Germany.

Lena Klein was nineteen when she fell in love with Jeremias Stoutenbeek. With the world at war and fear at an all-time high, there was a serious complication with her new romance. Jeremias was a handsome twenty-five year old when he was drafted into the ranks of the Nazi regime against his will. Lena Klein was Jewish. In 1942, after Jeremias had left Ludenscheid to serve in the war, Lena and her family were shipped to Buchenwald, a concentration camp where unspeakable medical experimentation was underway by scientists and doctors, under the watchful eye of the Third Reich. All that Lena endured was brutal, but she was strong and managed to survive.

Eventually, Jeremias Stoutenbeek was able to find out which camp Lena had been taken to and somehow finagled a transfer to this hell hole. He watched Lena every day that he could. A piece of him died a little each time he saw the visible effects of the horrific experiments being carried out on the only girl he had ever loved.

In 1945, Jeremias had been part of the resistance that had sparked an uprising, eventually leading to the liberation of the prisoners at Buchenwald. Lena was fragile but still alive, therefore was sent out on a train back to Ludenscheid. Jeremias also returned to his hometown and nursed Lena for two years until the experimental viruses the Nazi's had injected into her withered frame finally took their toll in 1947. The severity of her illness meant that although he was always by her side, Jeremias and Lena never physically consummated their love before she died.

I didn't have to explain a whole lot to Liz when we were finished. She had resonated with the cellular memory of life as Lena down to her core. The hurt was immeasurable, so much so that her body simply refused to allow any intimate connections; because it was waiting...waiting for Jeremias. Not knowing if the soul who had been Jeremias was even on the planet at this time, Liz and I both knew that carrying this burden another day would be completely counterproductive to her lifetime now. She held both Lena and Jeremias in her thoughts as I worked with the Solfeggio frequencies, 417 hertz in particular, to clear or 'cut ties' with her life as Lena. Cutting ties does not negate the lessons of an incarnation. Instead, it 'unplugs' an individual from the energetic drain and disruption that can be caused by remaining in the hamster wheel of a historical or parallel trauma. It's like closing an app on a smart phone. The information in the app is always available at the touch of the screen, but closing it down while it's not in use prevents the phone's battery from needlessly being drained.

Understanding this past life connection made all the difference in the world to allowing Liz to heal herself in present time. She is now free to connect with anyone she chooses at a deep level of intimacy that was previously unavailable, therefore, incomprehensible. In cases like this, there is often 'homework' to be done to retrain the body, as habits form to combat unknown phantoms. Liz had never experienced intimacy without debilitating tension. She would have to retrain her mind and her muscles to accept physical love with ease and joy. It was a habit she was very willing to break and a task she looked forward to with great anticipation for the first time in this life. Liz learned to use frequency in order to 'recalibrate' the habitual return to traumatic cellular thought patterns through repetition, allowing her brain to collapse old and recreate new neural pathways around her physical response to intimacy.

When Louise called my office for an appointment, she wasn't sure if she needed to see Mary Helen the Chiropractor or Metaphysician. She had sought the help of chiropractors, physical therapists, cranial-sacral therapists and her dentist. Following a routine dental procedure two years earlier, Louise developed an excruciating pain in her left temporal mandibular joint, or TMJ, as well as a debilitating pain in her left hip. Chiropractic 101 teaches extensively about the direct link between the two, but after exhausting the conventional reasons behind the relentless pain, Louise decided she had nothing to lose by exploring a less orthodox solution. Once a doc, always a doc, and with her particular complaints, I had to first check out the structural basics. Once I was fully convinced that the physical manifestation of these ailments was not due to anything in present time, I took my place behind Louise's head and asked... *"Take me to the origin of these issues."*

Almost immediately, the familiar buzz of time travel outside of the five senses kicked in. This sound always accompanies the 'mind movies' and I am certain that it is this instant change in frequency that allows me to access the information necessary to assist the people seeking my help.

Agreena Shirpnik was a bubbly, young German girl, just prior to the onset of WW2. She and her twin not only shared the same genetics, but the untimely misfortune of being born to Jewish parents during one of the ill-fated periods in history when Jews were tortured and slaughtered like animals.

I found myself remotely observing little Agreena's horror story inside of the Keiser Wilhelm Institute for Anthropology, Human Heredity and Eugenics in Berlin. This sterile and hostile environment was no place for children, yet the rooms heaved with the dishevelled and distraught faces of the unfortunate multi-racial children, or Rhineland Bastards, as they had been labelled and multiple sets of twins who had been rounded up like cattle for genetic experimentation. Agreena had watched her twin die right in front of her, unable to withstand the rigors of the dental research that she and her sister had been forced to endure. I could see plaster casts of teeth and jaws on matte metal trays around the room. Agreena was writhing in agony, her milk teeth barely gone and her adult teeth having been extracted without anaesthetic. Obviously, she was of no more use to her captors, with her twin having succumbed to the torture, dying of indescribable suffering. I cringed as I watched a phenol injection being administered into her delicate, young hip. She was gone within moments.

Back in this lifetime, two years earlier, Louise had undergone what would have been considered a run of the mill dental procedure to the average person. It appeared to have triggered a cellular link to a horrific event in Berlin, over seventy years earlier on our linear time line, in her life as a young Agreena Shirpnik. From that day forward, her body was on guard, waiting for the very worst. For some, it's a smell, for others, a location or an age. In this instance, an innocent trip to the dentist had triggered a tidal wave of emotion and pain. The piercing hip pain now had a perfect explanation; it had been the same hip in which Agreena had received the phenol injection that ended her life. Louise had been living with this mysterious pain for the two years following her dental procedure.

Agreena's horrific death had managed to manifest itself as iatrogenic physical trauma in Louise's present circumstances. Again, habits would have to be broken, somatic *and* psychosomatic compensations that had been made to accommodate the pain would need to be rehabilitated, but Louise finally had her answer and could get on with her life, now in possession of the tools to free herself from the chains of Agreena's suffering.

For some, pain or suffering, fear or phobia can disappear instantly. For others, healing and acceptance of the origin of disease becomes a voyage towards illumination. For all, understanding *why* is the essential ingredient that makes it all possible.

One Wednesday afternoon while working in Dublin, I was beginning to become very frustrated with 'the other side'. For whatever the reasons, on this day, information was coming to me at a much slower pace than usual; a snail's pace to be precise. A bit like trying to tune in to a radio station when you are out of range, things just weren't very clear and I had really struggled with my first two sessions of the day. I closed the door to the healing room, took a few deep breaths and reminded the powers that be that I was perfectly willing to serve, but I refused to scrape through another session.

I had eventually gotten all of the information necessary for my first two healings, but it had been like pulling teeth and I was prepared to pack it in for the day if the rest of the readings were going to go the same way. I acknowledged my own exhaustion, having just returned from a trip to America, participating in nightly rehearsals for two different events, and I was chauffeuring my girls back and forth to the many activities in which they were involved. I held up my hand, accepting that most likely the connection to Source was crystal clear, and it was my own foggy brain that was slowing me down. Whatever was causing the lag, when my next session began, it was as if a dam had burst. I barely had a chance to introduce myself to Owen before I could *feel* his anxiety coursing through my veins. Palpable, soul-destroying angst did not match the sweet-faced, mild-mannered man in front of me.

"I'm pretty sure I know exactly when my anxiety started. Back in 1990, I was visiting with my Mom, when out of the blue, she dropped dead right in front of me. She looked at me as she fell to the ground and there was nothing I could do to help her. She was gone. Ever since, I have had the worst anxiety, so bad, that it is tearing my family apart. I don't know how much more my wife can take. Two of my grown children are in therapy because they have watched me stress out over every little thing for so long, that they, too, have adopted this debilitating behaviour. I just can't go on like this."

Owen had attended another therapist that I happen to know, and after working with him, she suggested that there may be something else causing his incapacitating anxiety, other than the way his mother had died. He was willing to try anything.

Owen hadn't even made it to the table when the clear-cut images began to form in my mind. There was no static, whatsoever, in my communication with the voices as I shot back to southeast London in 1943. I was completely free of whatever had been slowing me down earlier in the day, as I steadily received the most horrific images of the death of the man Owen had once been.

The name Sandhurst Road School flashed into my head as a horrifying scene unfolded. Children were in the middle of school activities when a German bomber flew directly overhead and dropped its payload. I watched as a portion of ceiling collapsed on an adult male, presumably a member of school staff. He was trapped under the rubble, mortally wounded and unable to free his legs. It was as if I was now suddenly able to see the remainder of the vision through this man's eyes. There were children; the sweetest, small faces, screaming in terror as falling debris crushed their tiny bodies. This man could do nothing but watch in horror as these poor little children died in the most unimaginable pain, as his own life force slowly slipped away.

When I began to relay the story that had come through, Owen looked up at me and said, "This makes so much sense to me. If I hear of an accident anywhere in the city, I immediately call my kids (all adults) to make sure they weren't involved. It drives my daughter nuts, but I can't help it. The idea that something has happened to one of them and I can't get to them; *this is what keeps me awake at night*. I know it seems crazy, but for me, it's all too real. I also have an extremely irrational fear of flying. Maybe my fear of dying in a plane crash has really been a fear of being killed *by a plane* all along.

While Owen spoke, I went to my handbag and grabbed my iPad because the curiosity was killing me. When I plugged in the name of the school, every detail was there, right down to the report by eyewitnesses that the plane was flying so low that the swastikas painted under the wings were clearly visible. Owen and I looked at each other with excited disbelief. His feelings of helplessness now had a cause. The sudden death of his mother had not been the source of his anxiety...*but the trigger*. Watching his mother die as he helplessly looked on had awakened the recollection of this tragic event. The cellular memory of his death at the Sandhurst Road School had been a destructive force in Owen's present time family life, and now that he understood why, he felt like the healing had already begun.

Owen beamed as he exclaimed, "I can't feel a thing! It's gone! I'm telling you the constant anxious feeling I have in my body is gone! He hugged me at least three times before leaving the room. Ever so grateful that my own brain fog had lifted for this session, I wouldn't have missed this one for a million dollars, exhausted or not. To see the look on Owen's face, to hear the lift in his voice, to know that life may just become a little easier for this man...this is why I do what I do.

REFLECTIONS

With my hand on my heart, I say to you that I could write a novel the size of War and Peace about the souls I have worked with who have ties to the time period of WW2. With the political arena the way it is today, I could probably go ahead and start taking appointments for healing sessions in my next life time. Any time in history when a character rises to the surface, making a lot of noise along the way which focuses on separation rather than unity, you can be sure that major lessons are on the way; changes of epic proportions. Hatred, compassion, bitterness, empathy, racism, kind-heartedness; each of these and more are called to centre stage whenever a group of individuals rally behind a leader who does not encourage people to *better themselves*, but to attempt to prove somehow, that they are *better than* somebody else. Hitler managed exactly this on such a large scale, that all of these years later, there are still spin off factions of hate-mongers who more or less revere this man as a saint.

Now I'll endeavour to answer the question asked by so many of my seminar patrons, "Are you actually expecting me to believe that Hitler went to Heaven?" What I'm attempting to shed some light on is the idea that each and every soul who walks the planet serves a purpose. And with every fibre of my being, I do not believe in the literal fires of hell…period. Those who take the most difficult paths, the ones that require them to inflict pain, cause great suffering, force people to take stock in their personal responsibilities to fellow human beings, to express the deepest compassion, to share from the heart; yes, I am asking you to entertain the idea that these valiant souls take on the persona of Dark Knight or JAHO (Jack-Ass of the Highest Order) in order to create love from chaos. When we try to dissect this with our mortal intellect, it can become overwhelming, emotionally exhausting even.

When we connect with this concept on a soul level, it is easier to see that only the most experienced of incarnating souls to the Earth plane would agree to come to this planet to perpetrate such monumental change, in the form of an aggressor *or saviour*. To be honest, it never really works out well in the end for either extreme of the spectrum, does it? Taking on a role of that magnitude, to polarize completely to the dark *or to the light*, is an incredibly harrowing challenge for a soul incarnate. Some commit from a conscious vibration of service to humanity which often ends with tragic suffering and death, while others, I believe, do this because they are so deeply entrenched in the vibration of fear that only they could carry out such large scale atrocities affecting the lives of the population as a whole. These souls too, quite often exit with a dramatic demise. Those who are hovering in between, on a more personal mission, weaving their way through the darkness and the light, will have the chance to choose a path that best serves what they are here to learn. I feel that this is because of the massive energetic footprints created by the contributions of those who come here with the enormous task of affecting the vibration of humanity on a global scale.

There will never be a time in human history when every single occupant of our planet believes in the same politics, issues of morality or religion. There will never be one Messiah accepted by all of humankind, nor will there ever be one dictator who takes over the entire world. The population is too diverse, stages of soul development and soul plans too varied, and it is the ultimate insurance policy that any soul who incarnates here can have or *have not* the climate of love or hatred in which to grow.

Understanding this can ultimately allow us to view differently, the 'hows and whys' of a diabolical incarnation such as Hitler. He wasn't the first, and you can be sure he won't be the last. The potential fear and loathing with simultaneous benevolent humanity that can be generated by the rise and fall of such a figure is one of the greatest packages this planet has to offer.

When Money Matters

I have always found it fascinating that such an incredibly high percentage of people name finances as their chief complaint during a session. Of course, this isn't the primary focus of everyone who comes through my hands, but there are *that many* who consider themselves to be truly struggling, that I thought it was important to share. Money can often be the scapegoat for a number of reasons.

There are some folks who are unwilling to accept accountability for poor business decisions; there are some who were literally robbed by a business partner, lover, spouse, member of family or a friend; there are those who work their fingers to the bone yet can barely make ends meet and there are those who have no problem making money yet have the proverbial hole in the pocket, simply unable to retain anything they earn. I have come across a variety of reasons for money loss, actual scarcity and most often, poverty or *lack* mentality. The most typical ways for individuals to express their financial woes to me go something like this. *"I seem to have a block in becoming successful... I can't get my business to take off no matter how much effort I put into it... I am in a relationship I want to leave but I am trapped there due to our financial situation."*

In terms of past life connections, there are a wide variety of themes that surface around money. A 'popular' thread or course of study is where an individual is tied to an incarnation as a member of the clergy in a past or concurrent spiritual journey. Vows of poverty tend to frequently spill over into multiple lifetimes for a variety of reasons. These pledges carry a very distinct frequency and tend to hide out in the solar plexus and lower abdominal region of the human energy system. They are generally intermingled with issues of self-value and worth and if not dealt with, they can sabotage the greatest of efforts to make and retain money in the present embodiment.

Betty had been a practising psychiatrist for years. Recognised amongst her peers as one of the best in the business, she didn't seem to have the same faith in her abilities as her esteemed colleagues. Unhappily married, Betty wanted desperately to end her relationship and move on with her life. A huge mortgage, a car payment and a stack of bills meant that Betty felt that she was chained to the marriage, unable to conceive of a way out. (This is actually the number one reason given by people who feel they cannot leave a dysfunctional relationship). Betty's fear around money, her certainty that she would never be able to financially support herself outside of the marriage and the mountain of debt, had left her emotionally crippled and resolved to remain unhappy for the unforeseeable future. Yes, she had a few finances to sort, but her angst was completely out of proportion to the reality of her situation. *There had to be another reason.* I closed my eyes and waited.

The year was 1930, less than six months into the Great Depression of '29. Financial institutions had begun to crumble amidst the panic and hysteria created by the crash of the New York Stock Exchange. I could see a woman in her mid-thirties wrapping a rope around her neck. This lady had kept her life savings, $20,000, in the Chelsea Bank in New York City. When the bank announced its insolvency, wiping out every penny she owned, she saw absolutely no way out of a hopeless situation and hung herself.

According to the voices, this had been the fourth embodiment in a thread of lifetimes in which the soul was studying the inner workings of the human mind in relation to free will and choice. The objective was to create circumstances that would explore the impact of these choices made by an individual on the soul plan of another individual or group of souls. The voices explained that in this incarnation as the woman in New York,

Betty's current husband had also been the love interest who was *left behind* due to her choice to commit suicide. She had come to the conclusion that she was no longer capable of living after losing her savings. The cellular memory of the event had brought forward a guilt that was preventing her from leaving her husband in present time. Because she had created a death that was not on her original plan, one that was not a soul plan suicide but one resulting from overwhelm, she had chosen to incarnate, recreate the same feelings of desperation and present herself with the opportunity to find a different solution to her troubles. She could leave her marriage without leaving the planet and the soul who is playing the role of her current husband would also have the opportunity to deal with her departure under a different set of circumstances. It's genius really…the way it all works just fills me with wonder and awe.

For Betty, she now saw her situation from a different perspective and recognised that it was by her own design, making her feel far more at peace and in control of her life. She also realised that her calling to psychiatry had been no accident. For a soul who was four lifetimes deep into studying the inner workings of the human mind in regards to fear and stress, what better profession could she have picked? Instantly, she refused to allow money to dictate the path she would follow. Rather than being a slave to its influence in her life, she reframed her scenario and saw money as the valuable tool that had given her a new understanding of her own story. While she would ultimately end her marriage, she came to realise that she no longer needed the same excuses she had in the past. She was able to say and genuinely mean that the relationship had come to an end because its purpose was complete and no longer served her or her husband. To have the spiritual maturity to recognise this without having to point the finger, place blame or carry guilt was a game changer in Betty's life.

By all appearances, Johnny was the picture of affluence. Well dressed, extremely articulate and an expert in the field of finance, he had only one problem; he didn't have two cents to rub together. An absolute genius at giving others the advice and support necessary to keep their finances in line, Johnny had barely been able to keep himself afloat over the thirty plus years he had worked as an accountant. A walking contradiction, Johnny had the know-how and drive to be a successful businessman, yet a career-long series of misfortunes had left him penniless and working long hours to make ends meet, when he should have been happily retired, playing golf with his buddies. It simply didn't *add up*.

A client of Johnny's had asked if I could try to get to the bottom of this mystery. This man had not just been a customer but a dear friend of Johnny's over the years and he hated to see him constantly struggling. On a rainy afternoon in a small hotel conference room in Belfast, I met with Johnny. I must say, even though he was new to metaphysics, *gently persuaded actually*, he had a very open mind and was the first to admit that his circumstances were not a true reflection of the time and hard work he had invested in his accountancy business. Truly puzzled, he said he was willing to try anything to put an end to the constant battle with money. "Oh, and by the way, Doc, I've got this constant, niggling low back and leg pain that my own doctor can't figure out. Any insights would be much appreciated."

Ah yes, so often my 'whacky ways' are the last resort of many desperate punters…these folks also happen to be my favourite type of challenge.

Johnny hoisted his 6'2 frame on to the table, his good humour bringing levity to his current situation. He was in mid-sentence, telling me a joke, in fact, when I put my hand up to silence him. The voices had begun before I had a chance to take my seat behind Johnny's head. Not one, but three stories from antiquity began to unfold in a thread of lifetimes relating to Johnny's financial strife.

Scrooge in a toga… That's how I would describe the first man who appeared in my vision. Well dressed for the time, which appeared to be around the first century A.D., I could see a man who had tremendous wealth and stature in his community.

Unfortunately, this man's accumulated wealth had been the result of the suffering of others. A tax collector for the Roman Empire, he had been well paid and encouraged by the government to be corrupt. There was talk of dubious customs charges on the Jericho trade routes, which appeared to be his personal responsibility. In essence, this man had become wealthy by cheating others out of their own good fortune.

Immediately my mind raced to 17th century Scotland where Johnny had been a man named John Graham, 1st Viscount Dundee. Born into wealth, John Graham had mixed emotions about his stature and was more concerned with the fair treatment of the 'commoners' of the day. He served as a soldier under James VII of Scotland and eventually died on the battle field. Although money and the just treatment of his own family had not been an issue, Graham's morality had struggled with and fought for the rights of the common man.

My thoughts again were a flurry, as I next found myself in the middle of what looked like an old black and white gangster film remade in an explosion of colour. The Chicago bootlegging wars of the 1920's was the backdrop and I was now eavesdropping on a conversation between an Irish-American mobster and a Catholic priest. Dean O'Banion had a distinct limp from an incident that had left his left leg shorter than his right. (Recall that Johnny complained of a low back and leg issue). O'Banion appeared to be making some sort of deal with a Chicago priest, as in, the church was financially benefiting from the profiteering of Dean O'Banion and his gang. There was talk of a man named Johnny Torrio (I had never hear of him but later looked him up and found out that he had been in cahoots with legendary gangster, Al Capone). There was an air of justification as Dean O'Banion, being a good Catholic man, was *paying off* his beloved church to turn a blind eye, as if to vindicate his unscrupulous behaviour.

The pattern was clear. While I'm sure there were probably more lifetimes relating to this theme, particularly due to the time span, the three that were presented seem quite obvious to me.

From cheating tax collector, to a 17th century do-gooder, to the guilty conscience of a 1920's bootlegger, Johnny's soul had been studying the thread of personal values and how humans tend to rate themselves by their personal possessions. From at least several lifetimes, Johnny had been gleaning information about how destructive and constructive money can be, particularly when it becomes a measure of self-worth. Once he realised that he had spent his entire career (in this lifetime), beating himself up for his lack of financial success, he was able to conceptualise that quite possibly his coffers had not been overflowing *for a higher purpose*. When he genuinely stepped back and put his pride on the shelf, he was able to see the bigger picture.

Johnny was now clearly able to identify how he had been his own worst critic, putting himself down, literally devaluing his contribution to the world based on how much money he made. He gained a new understanding of value that day and suddenly felt very sorry for the way he had treated himself over the years. He had a home, a car and food on the table. No, he did not have as much as some of his associates in the business, but hadn't he made enough to learn the most valuable lesson of this lifetime? He was kind and caring and would give the shirt off his back to others. Johnny had the undying love of his wife and family, but he had not loved himself enough to consider these things the mark of a well-lived life. I think he found a new sense of purpose that day, and funny enough, when we caught up a year later, after he had taken the immense pressure to succeed off of himself, he shared that his business was booming and he was finally *making it big*.

☸

Amelia had barely said hello when she made a bee-line for the table that holds all of the tuning forks I use for frequency rebalancing in my healing room in Athlone. A passionate sound healing therapist, she was fascinated by the Solfeggio frequencies I often use to 'tune up' my clientele and couldn't wait to be on the receiving end of their healing vibrations. As Amelia gratefully rested her head on the pillow after her long journey from the south of

52

Ireland, she complimented the soothing colour scheme of the room just before mentioning that she had recently separated from her husband. She was on edge, unnerved by what this had meant for her financially. Although they were no longer living together, he still held the purse strings, meaning she felt he also still had control over her life as she struggled for independence. Amelia thought that fear of failure may be blocking her fledgling sound therapy practice from really taking off the way she knew it could. It had been a brave and risky move for her to leave the security of the marriage, but it was a risk she felt she had to take. So often I will hear from women over forty, that they feel as if they have no capacity to support themselves because they stayed home, worked hard to maintain the household and raise the children. I don't hear it as much from men or from millennial women. They seem to so easily forget what great feats they have already accomplished and that while they may not have been out in the work force earning a weekly pay check, the value of the skills that it takes to successfully feed, clothe and cater to the needs of a family are incalculable. Amelia sensed that her ability to personally succeed was blocked, feeling that something deeper than her present fears could be sabotaging her efforts. The voices were quick to explain.

It was Germany, in the early to mid-1800's. A surname I immediately recognised came to me; however, the *first* name was not one that I was familiar with. My days in physics class in Charleston, South Carolina suddenly came to mind, but when learning about Ohm's law, it had been Georg Ohm, not a man called Martin, who we had studied.

Martin Ohm was a mathematician and apparently the younger brother of the man who would forever be known for his findings in the field of acoustics, known as Ohm's Law. I was flooded with this individual's feelings of jealousy as I was told by the voices that Martin had always lived in the shadow of his more famous older sibling. Dynamic in the field of mathematics, Martin had never been truly acknowledged by his peers because the spotlight of scientific adoration was always on Georg.

I became keenly aware that when Amelia had made the courageous move to leave her failing marriage, it had triggered the cellular memory of her lifetime as the man who could never seem to 'make it' due to his brother's glowing achievements. Her gut feelings that something other than her present day anxiousness was responsible for this block in her ability to succeed were absolutely correct.

Ohm's Acoustic Law states that "a pitch corresponding to a certain frequency can only be heard if the acoustical wave contains power at that frequency." How absolutely perfect that well over one hundred years later, it would be frequency that would set her free. Her attraction to sound therapy, the use of frequency to heal on a cellular level, had brought her full circle to a different perspective of that which had been the bane of her existence in a previous incarnation.

When Amelia learned that Martin had eventually become properly recognised for his mathematical genius in the years following his brother's death, she equated this with the 'death' of her own marriage and suddenly felt as if the tide had turned. She no longer had to be in her husband's shadow. Just because he had been the bread winner of the family, her own contributions had not been unimportant. He had not been the block to her success, her own thoughts and feelings about her worthiness and capabilities had been the root of the problem all along. With understanding, healing can happen instantly, and after discovering the source of Amelia's past ties to unworthiness, she reclaimed her power and went on to create a successful name for herself in the healing art of sound therapy.

REFLECTIONS

There are a lot of old sayings about money, alluding to the idea that it is the root of all evil. The retort to these sayings usually justifies that money is simply an energy or tool. The way in which this energy is handled by the people who use it is the real source of 'good or evil'. I believe that the lessons which can be learned surrounding the good use, the abuse, the lack or abundance of money, are some of the most valuable. The very fact that so many fall prey to the illusion that their financial worth actually means something in the grand scheme of things is a good indication that the Multiverse deems lessons of the purse strings equally as important as those of the heart strings. Understanding the purpose of a thread or theme in the soul's long term plan can turn financial burdens into some of the most useful implements in the toolbox.

Addicted to Life

The Christmas of 2016 was seriously strange for me. At twelve and fourteen, my girls were humouring me each time I mentioned that Santa Claus was coming to town. I think I mourned the end of an era far more than they did. My explanations of the Spirit of St. Nick had been met with surprising understanding by Jada, my twelve year old, while her sister, Jemma, had been 'in the know' for the last two seasons. The girls seemed more concerned that things *look* the way they always had on Christmas morning. They wanted to be sure that just because they *knew* that Mom helped 'ol Santa out, that I would continue to create the same magical spread on Christmas morning. I simply pretended that I had no idea what they were talking about.

Another contribution to the weirdness of the holiday season of '16 was the fact that on two separate occasions, *within the same week,* two women, whom I had never met, contacted me to have *a chat,* one just before she was about to commit suicide, the other while seriously contemplating it. The first took place when I had taken my daughters to see the Nutcracker ballet in our local theatre. I can't begin to describe how bizarre this evening was for me. All excited to share this timeless classic with my girls for the first time, I think I enjoyed watching their faces almost as much as the spectacular ballerinas. My daughter, Jemma, turned on my phone during the intermission to take a selfie with her sister. In that ten minute window of time, a woman got through to me on her first and only attempt to reach me. I excused myself, leaving the girls to watch the second half of the performance with my friend, Rosaleen. I went into the stairwell to speak to this lady in private. She said that she had just finished my book, "Promised By

Heaven", and wanted to thank me for the peace it had brought to her. She was so tired; exhausted from being so totally different than everyone she knew and she was ready for it all to simply go away. It turns out, that she has had premonitions and visits from those in spirit for the entirety of her life. Her family, friends and even the parish priest had apparently been less than sympathetic when she foretold events that would come to pass within days of her prophetic dreams. She was tired of trying to explain that she wasn't crazy or possessed by the devil.

Picture me, sitting on the stairs, talking this woman around to the fact that there are a whole lot of people like her in the world, myself included. Now, visualize my face as 'Dance of the Sugar Plum Fairy' was tinkling away in the background as I'm talking this woman off the proverbial ledge. Talk about a surreal moment. It was an odd night out at the theatre, to say the least. And yes, after gently yet firmly reframing her *curse* for the gift that it is, this dear woman is still with us today.

Several days later, I got a phone call from a woman in the north of Ireland who is a friend on social media, but not someone I had ever met in person. To say she sounded dreadful would be an understatement. The despair in her voice was absolutely overwhelming. This highly qualified therapist had hit rock bottom with an addiction to alcohol and her husband had just informed her that he'd had enough. Her son didn't want her around his family and her husband had left home and text messaged that he may not ever come back again. Connie had decided that her family would be better off without her. She couldn't face the pain anymore and she no longer wanted to be the source of angst for those she loved. She had just finished reading my book, said that she had found solace in its words and felt compelled to reach out. She was feeling that if something didn't change immediately, suicide was her only option.

We spoke for about an hour and at the end of our conversation we agreed to meet in person the following week. Having just completed a very rough draft of the manuscript for this book, I emailed it to Connie to get her opinion. I kept my fingers crossed that this would keep her mind occupied until I could see her in person. I had the unquestionable feeling that there was more to her addiction than just being fond of a good bottle of wine. Fortunately, Connie remained on the planet until we were able to meet a few a days later and find out.

Her style and elegance was unexpected and did not match my vision of the utterly desperate woman I had first spoken to the morning Connie was thinking of ending her life. She was an enigma, really. Excellent at her work and happy in her marriage, Connie's compulsion to reach for the bottle simply didn't add up with the circumstances of her life. She even said this herself. Could there possibly be something else? A memory *from another time,* maybe? She couldn't get any lower, so anything was worth a shot. Connie described the urge to take her life as a feeling that didn't seem to belong to her. She wanted to live but it was as if an unforeseen force would consume her, pushing her to the brink of her mortal limitations. It was in these moments she would drink in the hope that it might dull the sensation.

Worn out from crying, Connie got on my table and closed her eyes. Only moments passed before the voices began to narrate a most disturbing 'mind movie'. *Inebriate asylum*...I had never heard the term before but was most intrigued, for some reason, by the combination of words. As the images played out, I found myself watching a series of elegant parties in the lavish homes of some of New York's upper crust during the mid 1800's. Mary Therese Dickinson, the twelve year old daughter of wealthy socialites was being handed an alcoholic beverage by an older girl who told her that she must learn to drink like a lady. Several scenes showed a very young Mary Therese quickly becoming the life of the party amongst her peers as their parents drank and made merry *more respectably* in the parlours and drawing rooms of the various high-end residences I could see. The movie suddenly fast forwarded to a twenty-nine year old Mary Therese. She had become a serious problem, an embarrassment really, to the family who had laid the foundation for her early onset alcoholism.

Before she had reached her thirtieth year, Mary Therese had been in and out of the New York State Inebriate Asylum on several occasions. Located in Binghamton, New York, the institution was the first of its kind designed to treat alcoholism as a mental disorder. At the time, it was en vogue to attempt to cure alcoholics with other highly addictive substances and brutal experimental medical procedures. During one of her tragic stays in the palatial compound, Mary Therese could no longer withstand the barbaric treatments. But more so, she could no longer accept the fact that her family, the very people who had fuelled her addiction throughout the years of social gatherings, had abandoned her; *Out of sight out of mind*. In 1878, Mary Therese Dickinson hung herself while at the asylum. The family did not come to claim her, going so far as to fabricate a story of her unfortunate demise while travelling abroad. Her body was laid to rest in an unmarked grave on the hospital grounds.

When I placed my hand on Connie's heart to bring her full awareness back into her body following a deep meditative state induced by the Solfeggio frequencies, she looked at me and smiled. "The darkness is lifting", she said quietly. "I can feel it leaving my body."

I explained to Connie exactly what the voices had said and the details my Guides had shown about her life as Mary Therese Dickinson in New York. As I spoke, Connie said that so much of this made sense to her in relation to the events of her current life. She had suffered with hyperthyroidism, swelling in her *neck* and the symptoms that went with the disorder. The fact that young Mary Therese had hung herself came as no surprise. Connie informed me that she, too, had spent time in a psychiatric hospital and that she had inexplicable and completely irrational fear of travelling to America...nowhere else, just America. Connie's countenance was changing right in front of my eyes. The effects were immediate and her relief was immeasurable. Connie now understood that her soul had created a similar set of circumstances in this life that would ultimately push her to recreate the same feelings of uselessness and abandonment she had felt in her life as Mary Therese. She had manifested the opportunity to face the darkness and make a different choice. In her personal life, this *knowing* would be metamorphic, in her professional life as a therapist; this understanding had the potential to become invaluable in assisting her patients.

I am happy to report that Connie has worked things out with her husband, has re-engaged with her son and his family and most notably, has not taken another drink to date. It is important to understand that we are all prone to repeating patterns or falling off the wagon so to speak. Connie's healing does not mean that she will never face the darkness again or be tempted to reach for a drink when the going gets tough. Connie now possesses an understanding of the origins of her patterns and therefore an unprecedented set of tools with which to face future challenges.

REFLECTIONS

You will notice that throughout this book, I refrain from using the term *healed* in favour of the idea that *healing* is an on-going progression throughout the span of a lifetime. It is a conscious act of participation in one's own life story with new perspectives and skills rather than an end point. We'll always face challenges; otherwise there is no point of being incarnate as a human. Understanding that healing is, in fact, a journey, rather than a destination can dramatically alter an individual's fulfilment and experience of life.

Living History

Recently, I was in Germany doing a few days of healing sessions for the friends and family of two of my dear friends. Ilona and Antje have not only enriched my personal story with their kindness and friendship, but have given me the opportunity to spend time in a country that has captured my heart since childhood. Both of these ladies act as translators for my non-English speaking friends in Germany. When my children and I travel to Potsdam and Berlin, we get the added benefit of the fact that each of these ladies grew up on opposite sides of the Berlin Wall for several decades. The opportunity for my girls to hear first-hand accounts about life behind both sides of the wall are priceless. Antje grew up in the west, and describes a very colourful and unencumbered life in *her* Berlin. Her father, a former archaeologist, wowed my girls with tales of taking his family into the heart of the city on that monumental day in November of 1989, when the wall came tumbling down. With hammers in hand, they symbolically took part in liberating their fellow countrymen from the east. This ageing 'Indiana Jones' captivated my girls as he passionately described what this day had meant to him.

Ilona, on the other hand, grew up east of the wall, where travel into the west was prohibited and life was much different for her than it was for her fellow Germans on the other side. Unable to bear another moment of the oppressive guidelines and strict rules enforced by the Communist regime, Ilona, her husband, Michael, and their young family fled their home via a daring car escape through the former Czech Republic border to Hungary and then Austria. They settled in west Germany until the wall eventually came down, allowing these brave souls to return home to reunite with family and friends. To experience another person's history through their eyes and perspective, to me, is one of the greatest privileges of being human. When one believes, as I do, that we are all part of the One, it brings home the concept of the Divine Creator's ability to be in all places at once. To share in the story of someone else's time here on Earth, even if only for a brief moment, is such an incredible blessing. It is for this reason that I encourage everyone to write or record at least a sampling of their personal stories. Journals, blogs, diaries and videos are excellent ways to give our loved ones in years to come, the opportunity to understand our current world from a more balanced point of view. History is full of misinformation and biased tall tales that often times don't even remotely resemble the truth, leaning more towards the perspective of those who held the power and the money at the time. The words of the people, not the government or the church, are where the precious nuggets of our collective past are to be found.

I am so grateful to know and love Ilona and Antje. These two powerful women have opened up a new chapter in my life as a healer by introducing me to the beautiful people of Deutschland. Ilona is also responsible for my cherished friendship with an incredibly gifted healer named Andreas Klose. Andreas shares his extraordinary healing centre in Potsdam with an open heart whenever I am in town. What a blessing it is to have friends who not only understand the intricacies of metaphysics but who so eagerly assist in facilitating the healing of the people of their native land by translating, creating space and sharing the love.

From Russia, With Love

Berta hid her distress behind a bright smile and a cheerful disposition. She was one of those girls who I found difficult to put an age on by appearance. While her outward features were fresh and strikingly beautiful, with silky dark hair, a stream-lined figure and the buoyancy of a care-free college girl, the abysmal sadness in her eyes told a different tale. At thirty-two, Berta was tired, worn out from the roller-coaster her life had become over the last seven years. She was a single mother dealing with a former husband who seemed less emotionally capable in life than their seven year old child. The instant recognition she had felt when she met her future husband while he was touring Berlin, had led her to believe that there's was a match made in Heaven; the return of a loving soul mate with whom she would live, love and grow old with after he re-located to Germany from Canada. She was a hard worker by nature, so when she began to notice his lack of interest in keeping a job or helping to ease her load when she became pregnant with their daughter, the worry set in. She hoped for the best, thinking that his apathy for contributing to their growing family would change when he held their child, maybe feeling the sudden surge of paternal instinct to care for his brood. Instead, he became more distant, detached from any seeming responsibilities, until finally, Berta had to make the difficult decision to leave the marriage and strike out on her own.

Rather than returning to Canada, the father of Berta's child lived off the German government, perfectly able, but unwilling to get a job in which he might have to give over any excess funds to his former wife. His moves were deliberate and calculated and he took the opportunity to disrupt Berta's life whenever he could, disappearing for periods of time then swanning in at his convenience, demanding to see the child. Wavering between protecting her daughter from this unpredictable behaviour and attempting to allow the young girl to get to know her father, Berta's heart was torn in two. His latest attempt to interfere with Berta's life had come in the form of a solicitor's letter, with intention to sue for full custody of the child. Not only did he not possess the financial means to see this threat through, he had told Berta that he didn't really want custody but just wanted to see her squirm. He had nothing better to do with his time...so he made her suffer. She knew that he didn't have a snowball's chance in Hell of gaining custody of their daughter, but he was willing to do anything to create whatever hardship he could. His actions were harsh and senseless. Berta had come to me with a very clear understanding that something else had to be the driving force behind this cruel behaviour.

I was well impressed with her knowledge that other life influences could be at play in this bizarre relationship and she was very interested to see if the 'instant recognition' she had felt when she first fell in love was actually a soul plan scenario. She wanted to be sure that she *got* whatever this lesson had to offer, so that they all could move on with their lives. Her understanding truly was remarkable and honestly, quite refreshing for me.

Candles were lit and soothing ocean waves played in the background as I first heard the sound of horse hooves echoing in the distance. The smell was musty and twilight was setting in. I was no longer in the healing room of the quaint city of Potsdam, Germany in 2016, but hovering over the streets of old Berlin, in the early 1800's. The tall and furry hats I will never forget. A band of Russian Cossacks rode into the city atop sleek and muscular chargers, oddly respected by those who huddled in the streets, out of fear, more so, than reverence. This elite, quasi-military fighting force of Ukrainian decent traditionally carried out raids against otherwise peaceful Jewish settlements across the Eastern European and Russian countryside. When they turned up in intimidating numbers to the city of Berlin in February of 1813, things became unsettled. The warriors had been warned by their own government to behave in a more reserved manner than their reputations as rapists and murderers allowed them, as they entered the civilised streets of the crown jewel of Germany.

While participating in the infamous Cossack raid on Berlin, Datan, a very proud, although inexperienced fighter met a beautiful, but very shy young lady named Ernestine. There's was an instant connection, a love so intense that it was bound to end in heartache. During the short yet passionate affair, Datan discovered that the beautiful girl with the soft, black hair and chocolate brown eyes was a Jew. The Cossacks had taught Datan to loathe the Jewish tradition, so much so, that he even denounced his own mother for her Jewish blood; the same blood that would forever flow through his veins. No one would ever know that he, a proud and pure Cossack was in actual fact, half Jewish. It had been bad enough that the first and only woman he would ever love was devoutly Jewish, but one fateful night, Ernestine made the grave error of telling Datan that she was pregnant with his child. Datan became enraged, knowing that he could never claim a child who had been born of a Jewish mother. He despised Ernestine for who she was and the choice she now 'forced' him to make. With one fell swoop of his blade, Datan sliced open Ernestine's belly and mercilessly ripped out her baby as she died a most agonising death in sheer terror.

Anything was worth keeping the dirty secret that he had impregnated a worthless Jew. Datan detested Ernestine as she lay dying, not only for her religion, but for getting herself pregnant and reminding him that he would never be pure. *He had no choice* but to kill her, and for that, he hated her even more, I shook off the dust of 1813 and snapped back to the present. I must admit, my heart was pounding just a little harder as I cringed at the idea of telling dear, sweet Berta the origins of her story. I steadied myself and proceeded to explain.

"The opportunity to experience this situation has once again presented itself under different conditions. Understanding that each Divine soul is simply playing a role in our movie, it appears that you and your ex-husband chose to come back to the same city to meet, in order to leave hints and reminders of what you were hoping to accomplish together. From two different worlds, you reconnected in order to grow through your differences. Just as he did last time, your former partner had the chance to see his child born, and under the present day circumstances, opted not to interfere with that progression this time. Once the child was born, however, the entire tone of the relationship changed and the idea of taking responsibility for his daughter was suddenly out of the question. Berta would have the opportunity to stay alive, to see her child born and to raise the girl according to her own value system. When the cellular memories of this past life were triggered for the baby's father, the obsession to see Berta suffer for 'trapping' him, not only culturally, but as a parent, immediately took over. Suddenly, the inexplicable and unfounded feelings of loathing had a cause.

Astounded by how easily she was able to resonate with her past, Berta sat straight up and started talking. Bits and pieces fell into place. Little details, such as her Canadian husband's Russian mother, began to make perfect sense; her feelings of imminent danger and foreboding when there was never a physical threat from her former lover. It all seemed so obvious now. There was a twinkle in her previously vacant eyes and it was clear that through understanding this piece of her past she would now be able to heal it. She was resolved, determined to apply this new knowledge to the current disdain she felt for her troubled husband. When she was able to visualise him as a loving soul who was only playing out a series of lives with her, surrounding a theme of intolerance and self-love, she had trouble mustering up any emotions other than empathy and gratitude for his ridiculous behaviour. She was now confident that in changing her feelings towards him, the entire tone of her dilemma would also change. She was visibly transformed by the understanding of her own story. This didn't mean that she would let him away with the bad behaviour this time around, but it did assure that her own emotional investment in their story together would change dramatically.

Her parting hug was lengthy, warm and full of promise. Berta took my hands, kissed my cheek and thanked me for coming to her country. Thanked me? I wouldn't have missed the chance to see the light in her eyes for all the roubles in Russia!

REFLECTIONS

My passion for people who live differently than I do has been the driving force behind my love of travel. This love of travel has in turn, provided me with the good fortune to work with people from all across the globe. One thing I have learned; no matter the culture, the colour or the conviction, the feelings invoked for any soul with a body, are exactly the same, no matter where they are from or what they look like. I love to facilitate sessions outside of my own country because after all of these years, I remain fascinated at how a country and culture are handpicked by an incarnating soul, to best serve the growth and understanding it wishes to obtain. A country with a history steeped in fear, separation and political strife can be the perfect playground for a soul seeking the experience of resolution of personal, regional or global conflict. A more laid back nation, one that has remained relatively neutral in the political arena, focusing more on the culture, arts and the care of the land can become the ideal arena for a soul seeking evolution through service and stewardship towards humanity.

The variety and texture of the lessons learned in Northern Ireland are different to those in my home in the Republic. The healing being sought by a Southern Californian, a Russian or German is also directly in proportion to culture and custom. In the end, however, no matter how different the wrapping paper appears on the outside, the gifts are all the same. Our cultural differences offer the most splendid assortment of avenues in which to express and challenge ourselves as dynamic and very curious souls. When someone truly embraces this idea, they are free to celebrate rather than fear those who are different to them. A lifetime of challenges, be they from a Nigerian banker, an Irish taxi driver, a Latvian restaurant owner or a Hollywood starlet, will always follow the thread that best allows them to experience every single aspect of what it means to be a person of colour, of wealth, of poverty, of integrity, of physical limitation or mental incapacitation, in the cultural circumstances and current judgements the present time in history has to offer.

I've said it before and I'll say it again; its sheer genius…

Non-Perishable

I am forever saying in my lectures or at book signings, just how grateful I am to have the opportunity to participate in so many people's unique life stories. Some lovely souls I only meet once, others I am part of their story for longer. Regardless of time, I grow and I heal a little more with each and every encounter.

Several years ago, I met Alexandra or Alex for short; the sister of a friend I had known for quite some time. Before she eventually came to me for a session, I had the opportunity to witness first hand, Alex's ever increasing anxiety. Having grown up in Galway city, she was well-travelled and had even lived for a period of time in America. Alex was a walking contradiction really; extremely witty, always ready for a chat, she loved a good time, yet she habitually put herself down and was fearful of so many things, that her anxiety could overwhelm her and become socially crippling at any given moment. Something about her just spoke to my heart. I guess in a way, I saw her as the poster child for the human spirit. Like "The Little Engine That Could", she never gave up on herself no matter how much she was suffering inside and always believed that the day would come when she would overcome her fears.

To this day, I find one of Alex's more unusual, troubling issues, one of the most fascinating stories I've ever come across. She had moved to Dublin to work in a city bank, a demanding yet rewarding job in which she was in charge of a number of employees who enjoyed working under her compassionate guidance. Her walk from the bus stop meant that she daily passed the gates of Trinity College, one of Europe's most prestigious institutions of higher learning. Out of the blue one day, Alex had what she described as one of her most harrowing bouts with anxiety, directly in front of the entrance to Trinity. The attack had been so severe that she had to call for a friend to come pick her up. She could neither continue on to work or return back to the bus stop under her own steam. She was literally crippled with fear and unable to move. It was this episode that finally prompted her to visit me for a session, in attempt to get to the bottom of her growing apprehensions.

Jolly on the outside but slowly dying inside, Alex could not see how life had brought her to this. Her job was going well, her health was in order and her family life was happy enough. Really, the only cause for concern was the looming recession, but this dilemma was one that everyone was facing and certainly not isolated to Alex or her family. Her husband had spoken about going to Canada where work in his field was plentiful. While she didn't like the idea of him leaving for a temporary stint overseas, she knew that this was a plausible solution to their worries and many of their friends were facing a similar prospect.

When I finally got her to relax and quiet the nervous chatter, I sat at her head and tapped in to her energetic memoirs to see what I could find. A tremendous explosion sent shockwaves through my mind as I could see dust and smoke coming up from the ground. Women and children waited in absolute panic to hear news of their loved ones, as my Guides informed me that I was viewing a mining explosion in Springhill, Nova Scotia in the year 1891. A woman waited for official word of her husband's whereabouts after learning of the unprecedented disaster, far from their home in the parish of Digby-Weymouth. Concerned parishioners gathered at the Trinity Anglican Church to await news... *Trinity*?

When Alex's husband had begun to research work in Canada, a trigger had been set into motion. In this lifetime, Alex's rational mind knew that if her husband went to Canada, it would provide financial security for the family, but when her energetic biography tried to process this possibility, the results sent her in to a state of sheer panic. The frequency of fear in her energy in present time had resonated with and matched her energy in 1891. It didn't matter what her rational mind knew to be true, to her energy body, this meant losing her husband the same way she had so many years ago. Her current intellect knew nothing of this antiquated tragedy, but her cellular memory had dragged forward the deepest memories of sorrow and death, innocently brought on by the combination of a suggested move to **Canada** and passing by the gates of a university called **Trinity**...the name of the church that Alex's *other* family had been members of at the time of the Springhill mining disaster.

Dumbfounded, I had to sit with my own astonishment at what had just been revealed. Amazed, yet again, at how the most obscure reference to something as innocuous as a name, could set off an avalanche of disparaging anxiety attacks well over one hundred years later in this unsuspecting soul. As gently as possible, I held Alex's hand as I shared with her what had occurred. It's at times like this when I am so grateful that it is me, an unemotionally attached observer who sees the past, rather than having the individual having to experience the trauma in their own minds. Typical regression usually sees the person go back to the event and can be quite effective in uncovering hidden truths for some. For whatever the reason, the people who have found their way to me over the years are generally very appreciative to glean the information that can set them free without having to recall the often painful details all over again. In the end, it's understanding the *whys*, the connection to the *feelings*, where healing truly begins... There are many roads to one destination.

Alex faced her fears and in the end, her husband did not have to leave the country. Through perseverance and a lot of letting go, she still gets a little uneasy at times, but has long since moved past the gripping anxiety that had become the predominant force in her life. Her willingness to go deep, not to mask over her pain and to actually deal with and release the overwhelming anxiousness that had become second nature, has given her a new lease on life. In the end, it was Alex who transformed her experience from merely existing to living large. By developing an understanding that the feelings she had never been able to explain were, in fact, not a figment of her imagination, she took back her power and continues to grow forward with great anticipation of how the remainder of her story will unfold.

When I shared the final version of this story with Alexandra prior to publication, we had the most insightful conversation after she had read this snapshot of her life. This conversation was so important, that I felt like it needed to be included because I'm all about *keeping it real.* I hadn't spoken to Alex for a while. Life had been busy for us both but we have that lovely kind of friendship that requires no explanation or excuses; we simply pick up where we left off. She said that reading my account of her experiences had brought her to tears. She complimented the writing and how it had moved her, but she said that some of her tears had come from the fact that only three weeks earlier, she had endured another panic attack; the first in a very long time. Feeling somewhat like she had taken a few steps back, I could hear the self-judgement creeping in. She started by saying it had been in no way comparable to the severity of attacks from the past and she suspected that it probably seemed worse than it was because it had been so long since she had felt that level of anxiety. I listened as Alex described her disappointment, believing that she had moved past these types of reactions to stress.

This is where my own history comes in handy. I teach and write about this subject for a living. I feel very confident in the contributions I am making to the world of metaphysics. I have joy in my life, a complex and meaningful relationship with my girls.

Overall, I feel very successful. Just this past summer, in a conversation with my girl's father, he said something that triggered a panic attack reminiscent of the kind I used to frequently experience when we were separating over twelve years earlier. He's moved on and I've moved on but something in the words, the tone and frequency of what he said, shot through me like a bullet and my body reacted like it had over a decade ago. I sat with it, allowed myself to feel it without judgement, and low and behold it was over in a matter of minutes. I explained to Alex that there have also been times that I have piled so much on my to-do list, that my body reached a breaking point and bang...a little panic attack came a callin'. I have so much going on, by choice I might add, that sometimes I forget to stop for a good, deep breath. If I catch a cold, or get a belly ache or a pain in my back, I'm the type who just keeps going. Every now and again, I push this body a little too far and it snaps me back to reality with a good old fashioned panic attack. This doesn't mean I'm stuck in the past, or hanging on to wounds from long ago. It doesn't mean I have failed or let myself down, nor does it negate all of the good in my life. It means that I have developed the knack for calling in a panic attack as a fool-proof way of getting my own attention. It 'aint always pretty, but that's real life; my real life.

I asked Alex to see this most recent episode from a different angle. Rather than judging her body's attempt to get her attention as something bad, I told her that if it happens again, to have an honest look at the days and weeks leading up to it. Is this, in fact, her body's way of getting her attention, asking her to slow down for a moment? If the answer is yes, then accept it, roll with it, feel it and then move on. Alex interjected at this point, telling me all of the massive positive changes that had taken place in her life following our session which outlined the origins of her panic attacks. She realised that she had immediately defaulted to her old script when this latest panic attack had taken her by surprise; the negative speak, the 'what ifs', the fear. I challenged her to write a new script; literally. I told her to take out a pen and paper and write down the major accomplishments, the valiant strides towards health and happiness she had made since the time when panic attacks were a routine part of her existence. I told her to keep a copy on her at all times so that if the feeling ever hit again, she could read out her new script, teaching her body that she has become someone different. It made so much sense, that I even took out a piece of paper and did it for myself following our conversation...just in case.

REFLECTIONS

Healing does not always mean that everything uncomfortable suddenly goes away. It means dealing with life's inevitable challenges in a way that honours your growth, celebrates your changes and accepts your human nature, unconditionally and with love. Understand this and see how quickly your feelings of value and self-worth will transform. One of the most unattainable notions for one who is suffering, either physically or emotionally is the idea of envisioning what life could look like beyond the present time affliction of the soul. Having a vision based on *hope* for a more comfortable life is **entirely different** to *envisioning* and *encoding* a new thought process that would actually allow for a higher vibrational state of being to come to fruition. One *begs* for a new reality…the other creates it.

Life's A Beach

No book I could write about healing would ever be complete without talking about the life enhancing adventures I've had over the years in Virginia Beach, Virginia. There is a detailed account of my very first past life memory *in this lifetime* in my book, "Promised By Heaven", (Simon and Schuster 2015). The short and sweet version is found below:

My family had taken a short vacation when I was around five to the coast of my home state of Virginia. I wandered away from our hotel as Mom and Dad were checking in. I became lost in the dark, by the sea, for hours. Rescued by the sweetest pair of hippies who had been camping near the ocean, I was eventually returned to my frantic mother, having had the best time of my life, while my father was still out scouring the beaches, fearing the worst. When Dad returned a few hours later, only to find me safe and sound at the hotel, he launched in to the obligatory lecture about how I could have drowned, all alone out there. In that moment, I flashed back to a memory that is as real for me today as it was over four and a half decades ago. A catastrophic event was underway; the world, as I knew it, was submerging under a colossal wall of water. I was in my early thirties, female and in charge of protecting a storehouse of information in the form of holographic symbols. I had, in fact, drowned all alone.

My five year old mind was suddenly keenly aware of the fact that this event was a real and extremely important part of my collective past. The fact that my father was scolding me about how I could have drowned; it meant nothing after reliving what it meant to drown in a wave of epic proportions, thousands of years earlier. My life was transformed that night but it wouldn't be until I was twenty-two before I remembered why. It wasn't something I ever thought about as the daughter of a Christian minister while growing up. In fact, I don't recall contemplating the concept of reincarnation until years later, when I would be reminded of this from an entirely different perspective; one from a bird's eye view of my body following a high impact collision that took me out of this world and into the space between lives. The veil of forgetfulness that accompanies us from incarnation to incarnation had been temporarily lifted when I was five. Following my accident, it permanently disappeared. I would never again forget in this lifetime that I had lived here, on Earth, over 13,500 years ago… and many times before and since.

My grandfather, Judge, had a profound interest in the great twentieth century mystic and healer, Edgar Cayce. When Judge was in his mid-teens, he had met Cayce in Lexington, Kentucky, curious to know more about how the incredible abilities this simple, yet enigmatic man possessed, were like his own. Judge had been grappling with *knowing* things before they happened, *knowing* things about people and he had a extraordinary healing energy that came through his hands. When Judge later became a doctor, he consulted on occasion with Cayce and remained a close follower of his work until Cayce's death in 1946. The circle of life would find me at Edgar Cayce's Association for Research and Enlightenment in Virginia Beach, over forty years after my past life encounter with my time in one of the numerous civilizations collectively known today as Atlantis.

I was in the library of the A.R.E researching the Arcturian roots of the Gotte alphabet, the ancient symbols I had seen as a child and saw again in a vision in my twenties. (I have come to realize that I have been carrying these symbols in my cellular memory for longer than I can remember). I was still laughing, following a morning session with the Egyptian study group, where the readings of Edgar Cayce are thoughtfully discussed by an incredibly eclectic group of folks. I truly appreciate anyone who can delve deeply into the esoteric while maintaining a brilliant sense of humour. I had been sitting next to just such a personality named Gail, when she suddenly piped up with " Hey, it's great that people seem to remember being priestesses and royals in these temples, but surely someone had to be in there cleaning the toilets?! What a perfectly insightful observation delivered with the comedic genius and timing of a pro. I absolutely loved the bones of her from that moment on. The cutest little giggle came from behind a laptop where the lovely Alison was taking notes for the group. An instant exchange of light between us was all we needed to remember that we were simply meeting...*again*. Needless to say, we all became forever friends that day.

The man who had been sitting on the other side of me in the study group came in to the library where I was researching through a vast collection of rare books and sat down at my table. The connection was instant, over 13,500 years old, to be exact. The first thing Gary said to me was that he couldn't wait to introduce me to his wife, Janice. When we met later that day, just as I suspected, I knew straightaway that I had known her too. Gary and Janice were not only family in my life as Beset, those many moons ago in the technologically advanced culture of Poseid/Atlantis, they had been my parents. They immediately became family again, supporting me in ways that one's tribe only can. Their beautiful home became my base for healing, workshops and the place where I would continue to meet friends from my distant past. It was a true homecoming in every sense of the word. Gary and Janice continue to this day, to be my rock solid anchors on the eastern shore of America. I owe them everything for the faith, love and time they have dedicated to my life's purpose.

One thing that stands out about Virginia Beach and the surrounding areas is the large population of reincarnated Atlanteans and those who are in touch with vivid memories of their *unearthly* origins. A pocket full of crazies? I hardly think so. There are doctors, lawyers, theologians, military personnel, government officials, educators and healers from all walks of life who have found their way back to the verve of Virginia Beach. Opposites may attract but like also attracts similar vibrations and so many of the incredible souls that I have worked with there are fully aware of the reason they now call this enlightened space *home*. My own paradigm has shifted so many times there, due to the honesty and integrity with which these people have bared their souls, their memories and their personal quests to gather with others who have the same intentions. In each case I have encountered, they have come to this place to assist in raising the vibration of this planet. I wish I could share all of the stories of the Virginia Beach sessions, but that in and of itself, is another book all of]its own. I will, however, share the story of one of the loveliest couples I have ever known, because theirs is not only a fascinating insight into life in Atlantis, but a love story that has spanned millennia.

Endless Love

Have you ever met a couple that have something a little extra special; that *I don't know what it is…but there it is*? I believe the French call it 'je ne sais quoi'. Obviously they are in love, but there's something more, something deeper than that, something bigger than simply singing from the same hymn sheet. When I first met Jo Ella and Dan I was intrigued to hear the story of how they had met, later in life. Dan managed arts organisations, conducted church choirs, and had been a teacher as well as a performing singer. He also has a grown family from a previous marriage. Jo Ella has lived a very full and exciting life as a professor, an accomplished musician and performance singer, as well. It was music that brought them together in this life and as it turns out, it was music that gave them their start so many years ago.

In the healing sanctuary that Gary has created in the spare room above his house, I first had a session with Dan, the kind of guy that anyone would be proud to call father or friend. Kind, loving and ever so genuine, Dan had no specific requests other than to let it all unfold. "Let's see what comes up, kiddo!" He smiled and relaxed on to the table. His trust in me was endearing. Classical music played quietly on the stereo, so totally appropriate for what I was about to see. **The voices** came swiftly, as did a detailed series of images complete with schematics and diagrams. I struggled to focus because there was just so much information coming through. I tried not to let my excitement distract me from gleaning as much information as possible for Dan. What I saw was truly extraordinary.

The year was 13,419 BCE. Dan, or Jaceur, as he was called in that lifetime, was a frequency engineer from the domain of Tahn, in the southwest region of Poseid, or Atlantis as we know it today.

Not only did Jaceur oversee projects involving music and entertainment throughout the mainland, he had designed and engineered the chambers used for vibrational realignment and attunement, the most notable method of healing in that day and age. A detailed graphic of the healing chambers made its way to my notepad, as I copied down exactly what was appearing in my vision.

The room, roughly 12'x12', was constructed of large, smooth sheet quartz walls with a limestone-like base for absorption, all covered in a thin metal known as orichalcum. A grid of intricate coloured lights wove a pattern across the ceiling. There were objects sunken and flush in the walls that resembled some sort of speaker system. The most enormous purple geode I have ever seen was hollowed out, smooth and polished on the interior, perfectly situated in the centre of the chamber. It was named amytheos, was nine feet in length and was the 'bed' in which the recipient would receive the healing vibrations. Nine feet long...*interesting*. **The voices** said that the attunement consisted of a series of light patterns in sync with specific frequencies that would physically levitate the recipient on an invisible pillow of air, re-setting the frequencies of the internal organs as well as the auric field. Coupled with ozone saturation and the highly oxygenated environment of the time, this was how Atlanteans were able to reach considerable longevity.

Every twelve suns, the community would congregate in an outdoor amphitheatre. This took place across the nation, each theatre indigenous to the natural landscape of the region. As this description came through, I saw an image of a massive stage made of solid quartz, built into a hillside. It was apparent that Jaceur's native homeland of Than rested on top of a rich bed of quartz. I could only imagine the buzz in that air!

The show traditionally started at sundown and was well attended by families of all ages. Talent was shared between the five regions of Atlantis, giving an endless variety of entertainment to the population. Multi-dimensional 'films' were often shown for amusement and education. There was a real sense of celebration at these events, using high levels of frequency and light to create a multi-sensory experience.

Jaceur was in charge of these special occasions in the region of Than, but I was also made aware that his skills were such that he was sought out by all regional performance arenas to create the most spectacular visual and auditory presentations across the continent. I suddenly flashed forward to the north-eastern mountains of the region of Ware. It was time to pick up this story with Dan's wife, Jo Ella.

Jo Ella's glowing countenance enters a room long before she does. Charming and delightful as my mother would describe her, Jo Ella's air of optimism only enhances her physical beauty. She's one of those women you aspire to look like when you pass the half century mark and enter the glorious golden years. Just as her husband before her, Jo Ella was wide open to whatever information we would receive during our time together. The mind movie and **the voices** picked up *almost* exactly where I had left off with Dan. It was a year later by modern measurements; 13,418 BCE. Although raven haired and much younger than the elegant, more mature blonde in front of me, the enchanting lady called Sedara was unmistakably Jo Ella. My first impressions of her were not in the physical form; instead, I was looking at a holographic projection coming from a metal disc, roughly 3"x3", identified to me as a metal-like substance called pyrela with an over-lay of orichalcum. This Atlantean version of a CD, would have music lovers in an absolute dither if the technology was available today. The holographic projection came from the centre of the disc so the experience was both visual and auditory. I'd say we're not too far off it ourselves in the near future. No device was necessary to play the recording; the recording was the actual device.

Sedara was well known in her time, much like our own super stars of today, her fame coming from the type of music she created. Sedara was a Mery. In the days of old, Mery, which has evolved into Mary over many generations, was originally a title, not a name. A Mery held a very special place of honour in the Atlantean society, as did the Mery's up to, and shortly after the time of Christ. A Mery was a songstress; not any ordinary singer, mind you, but one with the ability to sing specific frequencies outside of the spectrum of the human vocal range, due to possessing two sets or four vocal folds rather than one set of two folds. The Mery's role was to *sing* a child into the world, matching the soul's innate and unique frequency as it transitioned from Spirit through birth to Earth. Mery's were present at all sacred occasions, particularly death, when possible.

Sedara was the first to make publically available compact tonal healing. This revolutionary design would mean that the Mery's ability to match frequencies would be translated into a format available to the masses. In essence, Sedara was a sound healer and her product allowed unlimited availability to healing tones and frequencies. This was different from the role of the Mery at a child's birth, as the personal frequency of a soul could not be replicated. There were specific frequencies for the body, however, and there were more numerous types of bodies in those days. Unearthly physical characteristics were common amongst newer incarnates from *other realms*. There were also specific frequencies for energies and emotions found in the mortal form. These were particularly useful to those who were new to the *human* experience.

There was no surprise when the engineer of Sedara's compact tonal healing discs turned out to be Jaceur. I actually had the privilege of remotely witnessing their first meeting at a performance in Sedara's native land of Ware. Mountains rolled down into the sea and her regional theatre took advantage of both geological features. Built in to the side of a mountain, the theatre boasted a stage made of a thickened form of silica that projected out over the calm, cerulean sea. It was behind the scenes and just prior to her sunset performance that Sedara first met Jaceur.

Many lifetimes later and so many years later in this lifetime, they felt the unmistakable vibration of one another's frequency. Jo Ella and Dan had found each other again, making their home together in a place so obvious, one where frequency and the vibration of healing love is the rule not the exception. Virginia Beach is such a beautiful setting for a story that has never ended; a relationship between two beautiful souls, born of frequency and light enriched by an enthusiasm to share their song of love with the world.

Old Habits Die Hard

Not every past or *concurrent* life story that presents itself is of someone who was the victim of tragedy, illness or wrongdoing. Quite often I find myself at the head of the table with my hands on someone who is carrying out a very dark series of events in order to grow from or create growth opportunities for others. At times like these, it can be the ultimate test of being present, without judgement, with someone you would rather strangle than heal, in order to facilitate forward momentum for the soul. Who am I to judge what another soul has come here to create? I agreed to assist and serve with an open heart. As the mother of two young girls, my time with a man I'll call Edmund, challenged me to step far beyond the boundaries of my personal comfort zone.

While in the U.K. for a weekend of sessions, a very sheepish, middle-aged man named Edmund came to me seeking help with 'getting his life back together'. His eyes were full of sadness, even when he smiled, kind of like the woeful eyes of a Basset-Hound. He was a biggish man, soft spoken, unshaven, and wearing a golf cap to cover where his hair used to be. His auric field looked dense, thick and murky. Edmund was up front, right from the start, about the fact that he had just spent over twenty years in prison. He had served his time and now wanted to clear the energy of his past. He also wanted answers. There was a sinister aspect to his personality that needed serious examination. He had spent two decades asking himself all of the *whys* and had come up with nothing other than he must be mentally ill, emotionally damaged or a simply a dark and twisted soul. Deep down, he knew that what he had done was horrifying and unacceptable. Edmund looked me in the eyes and said that despite serving his sentence, attending years of therapy in prison and having a genuine cognisance of right and wrong that he was struggling with *the urges* again. He felt that something else, something bigger than him was pushing him to give in again. He strongly felt that no medicine or behavioural rehabilitation was going to help him with what he described as an overwhelming *compulsion*. He was absolutely tormented with the fact that he knew these impulses were wrong but simply couldn't seem to control them. We seemed to be speaking in riddles, dancing around the pink elephant in the corner of the room. Edmund lumbered onto the table and I barely had my hands around his head when my mothering instincts kicked in to high gear, like a lioness suddenly needing to safeguard her cubs.

Edmund was a convicted paedophile.

"Do all things with love...even the least of them amongst you...judge not lest ye be judged..." Every verse I'd ever learned about non-judgement was whizzing through my mind. My heart raced as I forced myself to resist the instinct to pull away. "This is a being of Divine Love and Light." The voices did not stutter. With that, I calmed myself down and focused on my gratitude, albeit somewhat reluctantly, for the opportunity to experience whatever information this man's energetic biography would reveal. It took no time at all.

The air was stagnant and heavy, like trying to breath when taking something out of a very hot oven. It was noisy and the language was sharp, high pitched and angry. Heavy stone walls surrounded a prison of sorts. Everywhere I looked there was sand mixed with dirt which created a dust that hung thick in the atmosphere, clinging to the skin and creating a sense of suffocation for the throngs of terrified people inside the prison, which looked more like a modified cattle pen than a proper jail. Conditions were unbearable with desperate families wedged together like sardines in a tin can. I was able to discern that more than one language was being spoken; that of the captors and that of the captives. As the dust settled, the pictures in my mind became very clear. Aware that I had Edmund in my hands in present time, I was half expecting to see him amongst the cowering prisoners; men, women and children who had been taken as slaves by the brutish soldiers who were screeching at them like dogs. We were somewhere in the ancient Middle East. It was quite clear that the hostages were less than human in the eyes of their captors and by the distinctly different linguistics; they had been taken from their homeland and enslaved. I could hear screaming, women wailing as their young children were being torn away from them as soldiers egged each other on to commit violent sexual atrocities, one worse than the next. When I focused in on one of the guards, I found myself looking into the unmistakable stare I had seen in Edmund's eyes. He hadn't been the victim of these heinous sexual assaults; he had been one of the soldiers committing them.

In that lifetime, Edmund had been a Middle Eastern soldier who had taken part in the captivity of an 'enemy'. It was perfectly acceptable, encouraged even, by his peers and governing bodies, to treat his prisoners, particularly the children who were unable to fight back, as sub-human creatures good for nothing but being raped to death and tossed aside like rubbish. Edmund had experienced on a different plane, in the time frame that we would know as several thousand years ago, the beginning of this thread of study of the inherent nature of right and wrong, good and evil. Now, here he was on my table, a convicted felon who had served a large portion of his life in prison for sexual abuse involving children. *"The urges are overwhelming"*. Those had been his exact words.

This was a clear case of the role that cellular memory can play in creating a 'story-line' in someone's life. Having started this thread in a time, place and environment that did not frown upon the abuse of children in captivity, the vibration of these circumstances had re-presented themselves in Edmund's current life. He was truly struggling with a mind that knew that his criminal behaviour with children was so wrong, but in a body with a perverse sexual appetite that over-rode any sense of righteousness. Knowing what I know about the experiences the soul seeks in human form, while my heart ached for Edmund's victims, the children and their families who were forced to deal with his horrendous actions, I also knew that *nothing* could happen in their lives that wasn't ultimately part of their own soul plans. It's a tough one to swallow, but this spiritual law applies at all times, not just when it feels comfortable.

Edmund now had his *why*. I was diligent in my delivery of this information as the source of a cause for his actions, not an excuse for them. We 'cut ties' with the old energy and worked on clearing their impact on his life in the twenty-first century. My hope was that he would take away this new understanding of his soul's attempt to grow through these overwhelming desires and build an emotional discipline that would see his light over take his darkness, but he would be the one who would ultimately have to shoulder this responsibility. Free will and the illusion of time with the promise of future/past/present circumstances working concomitantly would only tell. With love in my heart and a completely altered perspective, I wished Edmund all the best and prayed for peace in his heart as he walked out the door.

When I flew back home to Ireland, it was late when I returned and my girls were already in bed asleep. I sat for a very long time and just looked at them; small, innocent and full of expectation for a happy life. No parent ever wants to see harm come to their children. After all, I had been raped as a teen and my own parents eventually had to digest the indigestible. Yet, after all that I have witnessed, while I wish for my children deep and meaningful lessons that come with ease, I know this won't always be the case. I have experienced pain and hardship alongside joy and abundance, just as my children will. To support, love and cherish one another as we face adversity *and* delight is a challenge that we all have to face each and every day. In the end, it is most valuable to remember that no matter what life throws our way; no one can actually harm who we really are. It's in moments such as these, that we move closer towards understanding that mercy is the compassion we can show another human being, regardless of whether *we think* they deserve it or not.

REFLECTIONS

Struggles are inevitable to the human condition. Whether we make the choice to use these occasions as the building blocks of a solid foundation or the prison walls of life as a perpetual victim, is strictly up to us. We are the creators of our own stories and therefore have accepted on a soul level that *nothing we can do* or *nothing that is done to us* is ultimately for anything but our own highest good. *Nothing.*

PART 2

Not until each loom is silent
And the shuttles cease to fly
Shall God unroll the pattern
And explain the reason why
The dark threads are as needful
In the Weaver's skilful hand
As the threads of gold and silver
For the pattern which he planned"

-Anonymous
(The most cherished poem of my very first librarian, Mrs. Kesler)

Physician Heal Thyself

One of the most precious moments I've encountered along my own path of healing occurred when I was in the loving care of a most humble and extraordinary healer of Native American heritage, just a few short years ago. Under swaths of soothing turquoise silks rolling gently across the ceiling like the lapping waves of a calm, Caribbean sea, Sharon spoke softly as she sat behind me, her hands gently cradling the base of my skull. I was weary and had come for respite in her healing sanctuary, which recreated the serenity of a beach front cottage with inviting, sea green, wood plank walls and a heated, water bed plinth. I had just come off a marathon run of facilitating healing sessions and had given everything I had to assist these fellow 'humans being' through the trauma of some intensely complex physical and emotional challenges. In short, I was spent.

When my session came to an end, Sharon revealed that she had a very important message to share, one that may assist me when I found myself in danger of depleting my own energy while attempting to help another individual to heal. "There is a beautiful sentiment by Godfrey, a Lakota Indian Medicine Man, which I think you should keep in mind as you work, MH. He said of himself, "I am the spirit's janitor. All I do is wipe the window a little bit so you can see out for yourself." Sharon went on to tell me that as healers, we are but window washers to the soul, wiping clean the muck and grime accumulated by life, so that the person before us might clearly see what is right in front of them, thus finding their own way home.

"It's not about how much *you* give, darlin', it's about getting out of the way, allowing your gifts to flow unencumbered, providing just enough insight for these folks to rediscover their soul's plan and come up with their own answers."

My paradigm shifted, yet again, that day, as well as the way I would serve.

Ghost in the Machine

Hardwood floors, plank ceilings, thick cottage walls and an open, stone fireplace; sounds like the inner sanctum of my local pub. But no, this was our new home. Situated only a few miles outside of Athlone in the picturesque village of Brideswell, my girls and I had relocated to the solitude of the Irish countryside, complete with a garden adorned by apple trees, the obligatory stone walls and rolling green fields. I guess I had become quite fond of the sheep, as they were now my neighbours, along with the cows, horses and occasional donkey.

Built in 1912, the house had belonged to Mr. George Burke, and as far as we were concerned, it still did. Renovated and restored to its former glory, our new neighbours, Dermot, Anne Marie and their son Shane, had worked tirelessly to recapture what every antiquated, white-washed farmhouse could hope to be- authentically Irish. I mourned not only the loss my relationship with the girls' father, but also the loss of the palatial family home that we had designed and built a few years earlier. I now looked around and embraced the idea of 'Home Is Where the Heart Is'. I was flying solo now. Not only was I an American living out her childhood fantasies of rainbows and fairy forts, I was living in a quaint, Irish cottage that came with a little something extra. *Mr. Burke....*
When my kitchen light began to flicker on the evening of August 7th, 2007, I figured Mr. Burke, our resident spirit and the previous owner of our new home, was just saying hello, *or that I needed to change the light bulb.* From the first day had we shifted our belongings in to the picturesque, Irish cottage in the country, we had been greeted by the smell of turf fires when no fire was lit, moving furniture when no one was moving it and footsteps up and down

the hallway on any given night. Music would often play quietly out of nowhere and on numerous occasions, my two little girls would see Mr. B standing at the foot of their bed. They saw him, could describe him down to his last whisker, and they simply adored him. After their father had left the country, Mr. Burke had become the new man in our lives, *body or not*, and quite frankly, this was my dream relationship. A male presence with no commitment required! The girls would run through the back door every time we arrived home shouting, "Hi Mr. Burke, we're home!"

I know, I know...some future therapist is going to put their kids through college on this one!

On this particular night, however, Mr. Burke wasn't up to his usual antics; we had a new visitor. Not long in the door from a weekend away in the wild west of Ireland, my friend Tanya and her daughter, Kaci, were staying the night before heading back to County Longford the following morning. The girls were all in bed giggling, having an absolute ball. They were enjoying that lovely time in childhood when the grown-ups are none the wiser that flash lights are on under the blankets and sweets are stashed in the pillow cases. The girls felt safe and assured by our voices in the kitchen chatting over a cup of tea, however, what they were actually hearing, was no ordinary chat.

The kitchen table was covered with colourfully wrapped presents that had arrived in a package from the girls' dad. He had been gone from Ireland for well over a year. His job as a marine engineer took him to all sorts of interesting ports of call. Tanya remarked that the gifts had reminded her that it was, in fact, her own Daddy's birthday.

Tanya's father, Sean, had been killed in a car accident in November of 1999. She still grieved the loss.

"After all of these years, I still can't believe he's gone."

The light began to flicker as we stared at each other with the "Did you see that?" look. Not only did we see the light, we also saw two other lights. Tanya had two mobile phones, one for personal use and one for business. One sat on the kitchen counter and the other between us on the table. Both phones lit up simultaneously. They were flashing on and off, yet not ringing. And then we heard it; a mechanical voice coming through one of the phones.

"I am here..."

"Sweet mother of divine! Mary Helen, did you hear that?"

"I am here... Proud of you..."

Now, I don't get spooked too easily. Are you kidding? With the life I've led?

I was totally freaking out!

I had heard of the electronic voice phenomenon on those zany ghost hunting shows. Sounds picked up with high-powered microphones as some wide-eyed celebrity host whispered closely into the camera to the at-home audience, as if they were right there in the dank, dark cellar of some ancient, English castle. I had heard of it, but I had never actually *heard* it.

With every hair standing on end, we grabbed a crystal pendulum and quickly asked to be shown the direction for yes, then no. With a voice trembling with excitement laced with a little dash of terror, Tanya asked, "Sean...is that you?" The pendulum began to swing wildly in the direction of yes.

Lights still flickering, my eyes welled up as I watched and listened to Tanya's daddy communicate with his little girl. This was a huge moment for me. On so many occasions I have delivered messages from the other side to people who sit in shock, awe and sometimes horror, as friends and relatives make their presence known. At first, it is a leap of faith, until inevitably the spirit uses some obscure piece of information that I couldn't possibly know, to let their loved one know, *"Hey, it really is me."* To watch someone else hear it and see it for themselves was a pivotal point in my experience as one who converses with those in spirit. Believe it or not, having this gift can be a little lonely at times. To observe the story as opposed to being the one telling it was a rare treat for me. In some way, it validated my own struggles with the ability to hear spirits over the years. As cool as some think this skill is, there are equally as many who think something else is afoot. A little cray cray? Delusional? Playing with the dark side? Luckily, I am not really bothered by other people's opinions; however, a little piece of me was relieved when this soul chose to share his voice *outside* of my head. A decade following his death, Tanya was gifted with the chance to spend one last birthday with her Daddy. Really, there are no words to describe her elation that night.

Less than a month later, I was going through some photos on my laptop of a trip I had taken in June to Martinsville, Virginia, my home town in the U.S.A. I had been delighted to hear that my parent's next door neighbours, the McClains, were at long last, planning a trip to Ireland. Charlotte and Alan had seen as much of me in their house as my parents had in my own home when I was a child. They had one son, Brother James, my Dad called him. I was his babysitter, and I loved him as if he was my own little brother. Charlotte had been my piano teacher from the day I had been tall enough to reach the keys. It was no easy task, because even as a child, I would rather socialize and *hated* to practice. I was a true source of frustration. Charlotte would get me to stand across the room facing the wall while she would play random notes on the piano. She quickly had discovered that I had perfect pitch, the ability to pick out any note on the keyboard and identify what it was, only by hearing the tone. What a waste, I'm sure she thought, but to this day, I can assure her that the talent didn't go unused. Listening to the delicate harmonics of the human energy field is a far cry from learning to play the classics. Nonetheless, her years of hardship with her most challenging pupil certainly paid off. I am able to hear minor discrepancies in a person's electro-magnetic frequency that helps me to pinpoint physical and energetic dysfunction within the system. Roll over Beethoven!

During most of my trips home, our schedules never seemed to match up for anything other than an all too brief catch up. This time, Charlotte and I both found a day that we were free and decided to spend an afternoon in the town's Museum of

Natural History. A great feather in the cap of the former furniture capital of America, Martinsville was home to the research facility for archaeological finds from around the great state of Virginia, including several large dinosaur bone exhibits.

A display of the history of the American Indians native to the region was currently the main attraction. As an ambassador for the community, Charlotte was so proud to show off the museum's latest addition. I took several photographs, including a lovely one of my dear neighbour in front of a magnificent reproduction of a Native American wigwam.

Back in Ireland, I had pulled up the photos on the laptop that I had taken in June, and was showing them to my girls. I had just gotten to the picture of Charlotte posed in front of the wigwam when I went to click on to the next picture. It wouldn't budge. I wasn't prepared for what came next.

"Don't be afraid, his time is here. Don't be afraid his time is here." The mechanical voice spoke rapidly, saying the same words over and over.

"The *'umputer'* is talking, Mommy!" Three year old Jada squealed, excitedly.

"Why won't the picture of Mrs... *What's her name again?*"

"Mrs. McClain, Jemma, that's Mrs. McClain." I murmured to my puzzled five year old, with a sense of foreboding.

The robotic words kept repeating. I ran upstairs, two at a time, to grab my digital recorder, praying that this voice wouldn't stop before I made it back down. The girls were screaming, as they had now deciphered what it was saying.

"Whose time is here, Mommy? Why is it telling us not to be afraid?"

It was Sunday evening, September 2nd, 2007. I looked at the clock and subtracted five hours, wondering if Mom and Dad might be home from church yet. I had now recorded the voice and it continued to repeat its automated warning as I placed the call.

"Hello?" Mom answered, chipper as always.

"Hey Mom, it's me. Quick, have a listen to this!"

I held the phone up to the computer and let her listen to the eerie phrase at least ten times over.

"My heavens, what in the world is that?"

"Mom, you're not going to believe this, but the computer has frozen on a picture I took of Mrs. McClain this summer, and a weird, mechanical voice is now talking through the speakers!"

"Did you record that voice on the computer?"

Bless her heart...Mom had only just begun to experience the phenomenon of email and had absolutely no idea how a computer worked. I can't say I was too far ahead of her, but this I did know. This was a still photograph, not a video, and the motorised voice was reminiscent of the one I had heard only weeks before, when Tanya's deceased father had spoken through her mobile phone speaker. Something inconceivable was taking place.

"I can make out *afraid*, but I can't hear the rest very clearly." She said, still baffled.

"Mom, its saying don't be afraid his time is here!"

"Oh my, *his* time? Do you think it's talking about Alan?"

"I sure hope not, they're supposed to be coming over in a few weeks!"

"Oh my gosh, what should we do?" The concern was growing in her voice.

"There's not a lot we can do, Mom. It's certainly not the kind of thing you call up and casually drop on them."

"No, it certainly isn't."

By the time we had finished the conversation, the voice had stopped.

"Well girls, we need to say a special prayer for the McClains tonight. Things might be changing for them soon." I snuggled up with the girls, trying my best to explain the inexplicable.

"Is Mr. '*Aclain*' gonna die, Mommy?" Jada asked in a sad, little voice.

"That's in the hands of the Creator, honey, and remember, *we* are the creators of our soul's plans here on Earth. All of us are born, and all of us will return back to Spirit. Some of us just go a little sooner than others. You both need to understand that part of being *who we are* sometimes means seeing things or hearing things before they happen. Some of these things can be wonderful, while others can make us feel very sad, especially when its news about someone we know and love. I want you to know, it's *never* something you need to be afraid of. We have been given a very special gift. Your great-grandfather had it, Grandma has it, I have it and you both have it. Sometimes for you and me, knowing when people are going to leave this world is a part of our gift."

"Well they can keep it!" Jemma cried.

"I don't want to know unless it's nice! What if some voice tells me you are going to die? Or Jada?" She buried her little face in my chest and sobbed.

I empathised with her concern. I had known the circumstances surrounding my own death and the deaths of my parents since I was younger than her. Sleep did not come easily for any of us that night.

The following day, I arrived in to work and played the eerie proclamation I had recorded for my office manager, Maureen. Well-seasoned after years of dealing with my 'weirdness', as she called it, she listened intently. I asked her to tell me what she thought it was saying.

"Don't be afraid, *the* time or *his* time is here." She listened on with a slight look of horror.

Our friend, Mick, was visiting the office for a cup of tea and a chat. A former guard (Irish police officer) turned private detective, Mick also listened to the recording with his well-trained ear.

"No, that's saying "Don't be afraid, *his* time is here". I'm certain of it." Mick folded his arms and crossed his legs, confident with what he had just heard.

On Thursday morning, September 6th, our dear friend and neighbour, Alan McClain, passed away. Mom hardly knew what to say when she rang. She didn't really have to say anything. Always positive in her outlook, she expressed how grateful she was that he had died at home.

"Can you imagine how awful it would have been if they had been crossing the Atlantic or already in Ireland? That would have been so much more difficult for Charlotte and James to deal with."

When giving my condolences, I told Charlotte that I had loved Alan dearly and was blessed with wonderful memories of this truly great individual. I recounted his sense of humour, the amazing parties they threw during my childhood that centred on his extensive and incredibly sentimental electric train set. I especially remembered that he always had time for me. That's what meant the most. I've said numerous times in the past, *just because you know, doesn't make you immune.* Death no longer has the same sting after having my own temporary demise, but my heart still hurts, every single time I lose a character from the story of my life. This passing was particularly tough, as I now had to break the news to my little girls. They hadn't known him well, but had seen him every time they had visited their grandparents in America. They were none too happy about the fact that they knew it was coming. They both cried that it just wasn't fair.

I knew exactly how they felt.

The Queen Scary

I was invited to speak a few years ago at a conference on board the illustrious and mysterious Queen Mary, which is permanently docked in Long Beach, California. If you have a few spare moments, Google the Queen Mary and read up on its amazing history as a luxury cruise liner in the 1930's, come troop carrier during WW2, retired to shore in the late 1960's. Many a movie star and dignitary graced her majestic decks and she is full of tales of ghostly apparitions and supernatural phenomenon, adding to her haunting allure and mystique.

From the moment we stepped on board, it was like being sucked into an outlandish time warp. I had travelled with my dear friend and agent, Mairead Conlon, and another Irish friend who had wanted to come along because she had never been to LA. The décor of the ship has been maintained from its heyday, right down to the impressive variety of wood wall panelling, opulent chandeliers, original toilets and cast iron bath tubs complete with original salt water taps. She truly is a sight to behold.

The day after I arrived, I was asked to be a guest on a radio show that was being broadcast that evening from the ship. As this episode on the paranormal came to a close, the hostess finished up by asking me if I had experienced anything unusual since my arrival on the Queen Mary. In all honesty, all I could say was *No*. Up until that point, absolutely nothing untoward had taken place, except the terrible sinus problems I had developed over night, which I was putting down to the re-circulated air on the 11 hour plane journey from Ireland to LA.

No sooner than the statement had left my mouth that I had seen nothing out of the ordinary, the spirits decided to make a monkey out of me! I was standing by the doorway into the adjoining room of the splendid and stately suite where the show was being broadcast when all of a sudden, a light flashed, much like the old- timey light bulb flash of a vintage camera. It was bright and made a popping noise. I looked at the other folks in the room, hoping they had seen it too. Not only had they seen it, but we all noticed the sudden drop in temperature in the bedroom as compared to the sitting room, where we had spent the last hour chatting, live on air. I giggled and passed comment that it could have at least flashed BEFORE I made the declaration on international radio that nothing strange had happened to me aboard the world's most haunted ship. Little did I know, the fun was only getting started.

I said my goodbyes as I entered into an endless corridor of identical antique doorways. With everything in its original state, it was like stepping out of a portal into the golden days of maritime travel. Left looked just like right and I wasn't sure which way to go to get back to the lobby of the colossal ship. I eventually went left and found myself walking past door after door of infinite cabins and hidden walkways. I took another turn and suddenly realised I wasn't by myself. You know that feeling when you *know* you're not alone? When you can actually feel someone in your space? Not only could I feel it, but I heard giggling, just as I turned around to see a little girl following me down the hall. She wore a drop-waist white dress with pleats at the bottom and a very large bow in her hair. She laughed because she *knew* I could see her; I joined in her merriment because *I knew that she knew I could see her, too*! Why so strange? This child had drowned in the ship's swimming pool during a voyage with her family, well over half a century earlier.

I went up to my room (the second room that we had moved to because the first room we had been assigned was like an ice-box) My friend and I made our way up to the Observatory Bar, a beautiful example of classic art-deco design. We settled down for a bite to eat and a chat. I was telling her about my earlier escapades with the little girl in the corridors when a man behind her in the far corner of the bar caught my eye. It wasn't his dashing good looks that commanded my attention, but the look of sheer surprise on his face that I had noticed him. I couldn't help but stare, as he stared right back. Dressed in a tan coloured maintenance man's uniform and as *in the flesh* as every other live person in the bar, I nearly choked on a tortilla chip as he stepped left and went straight through the wall and out to the observation deck. Before I could tell my friend what was happening, the man leaned back through the wall with only the upper half of his body; as if to let me know that I wasn't just 'seeing things'.

It turns out that back in the day, there had been a fire drill on the ship and a worker had been accidentally crushed to death as a water-tight door was sealing shut. Oddly enough, I didn't get the sense that it was the man who had been killed that I was seeing. I felt like it was the man who had unwittingly been responsible for his co-workers untimely demise who was staring me in the eyes.
Cue creepy music....

On the Saturday night of the three day conference, a ghost tour had been organised for some of the seminar participants and guest speakers. The loveliest man had come along with a satchel full of ghost hunting equipment, including a device that converted frequencies into phonetics, allowing a spirit to communicate with those who don't have the ability to hear them without assistance.

My Irish friend, who had travelled with me, had become quite the paranormal photographer, taking some amazing pictures of orbs around the QM. One photo, which had been taken down in the bowels of the ship, clearly showed a man in a cap and a young girl with a big red bow in her hair. When we were in the boiler room, reputed to be *the* hottest hot spot of paranormal activity, our ghost hunter, John, was picking up a lot of clatter on his EMF devices. He was so gentle in his attempts to coax the spirits to move in to the light, telling them that they were loved; that it was safe for them to return home. He was so sweet in fact; it was not only endearing, but comical. Anyone who knows me is well aware that I don't fare well in situations where I am supposed to act serious, especially when something funny is afoot.

"You are loved, all is safe and well, you can move into the light now, you are beautiful, we all love you!" John gently continued to coerce the spirits. I was childishly snickering in the corner. It struck me so hilarious, I simply couldn't help myself!

As he continued to compassionately guide these lost souls, the EMF box made a very distinct clamour. I stopped dead in my tracks and said, "Did that thing just say what I think it said?" I was now in the horrors of laughter as John's jaw dropped to the floor. Much to my relief, he began to laugh heartily too!

In response to John's sincere and polite commands, a mechanical voice had spoken out; *very clearly I might add*, from one of his devices. Somewhat reminiscent of the unmistakable robotic communiqué of scientific genius, Stephen Hawking, the box loudly squawked back,

"F*#@ YOU!"

I nearly collapsed.

The following year, I had the opportunity to revisit her majesty, Queen Mary. This time, I was delighted to bring my favourite travel companion along for the adventure. My mother, Momma Helen, is the most elegant and lively 89 year old southern belle and is every bit as regal as the Queen Mary, herself. I couldn't wait to get her on board to see what kind of antics would unfold. I was speaking at another conference and was delighted to be back with my dear friends in L.A.

On the previous year's trip to Long Beach, I had experienced a most unusual visitor one night after I had gone to sleep. I awakened to see a very palpable apparition standing next to my bed, simply looking at me. In his hands, he held a diamond necklace, the kind you would see draped around the neck of a Hollywood starlet in the 1940's. I asked this spectre if I could help him in some way. Apparently, he had only come to brag in front of someone who possessed the ability to actually hear and appreciate his story. He explained that in 1933, he had stolen this necklace from a passenger, when the ship had sailed as a luxury cruise liner, prior to WW2. That was it. No other message; just a spirit that wanted to toot its own horn. I found the visit peculiar and highly amusing.

Now, the following year, I was eager to see if my mother would get to experience any of the ghoulish shenanigans the Queen Mary had to offer. My lovely agent, my Irish Angel, Mairéad, had travelled over from Ireland. I had flown ahead of her in order to stop in Virginia to pick up my mother, before carrying on to L.A. Mom absolutely adored being on the ship, particularly because the view out of our portal window was across the water from the oil rigs. This location had been the base for the Navy ship on which my grandfather, Judge, had been ship's doctor in WW2. Mom's family had lived near Long Beach for a short time when she was a child, so it was a special sort of homecoming for her.

Of course, I had told Mom all about the ethereal entertainment that had taken place on the ship during my last visit. She had been particularly intrigued by the diamond thief of yesteryear. When Mom and I crossed the threshold into our cabin for the first time, the necklace I had been wearing all day suddenly flew off my neck and landed half way across the room. Mom said it looked as if it had been ripped right off my neck and flung into the floor. We joked that the jewellery thief must be excited to see me again because once again, he had the ear of the girl who could actually hear him brag about his infamous heist!

Mom wanted to shower after the long flight so I went the two steps across the corridor into Mairéad's cabin for a cup of tea and a chat. About twenty minutes later I went back to my cabin because Mom was calling my name in an anxious/excited sort of tone. There stood Mom in her little shower cap and dressing gown with the strangest look on her face. "Did you do this?" She asked with a nervous laugh. "Do what?" I had only just walked back into the room and I had left it before she had even gotten in to the shower. "Look at this!" Mom was absolutely stupefied.

There, on the dressing table, Mom's tri-fold satin jewellery pouch had been unfolded, and her necklaces and earrings were stacked, one on top of the other, in the shape of a Christmas tree. She had brought a necklace to wear that was an old show-jumping medal, made of gold filigree, dating back to the early 1900's. The delicate chain, which had been sealed in a separate zip-lock baggie, was now wrapped around each intricate, hand-crafted letter of the medallion, with absolute precision. The hairs on the back of my neck stood on end and I was over the moon that the paranormal activities were wasting no time getting under way. We had only been on board for a couple of hours!

Mairéad came flying into our room when she heard all of the commotion. It was then that she declared on the spot, "I want absolutely nothing to do with anything spooky, scary, ghostly or paranormal while I am on this ship! I'm not kidding!" She was now yelling at the ceiling while Mom and I were in the knots of laughter. She walked out our door, made an exaggerated wave of the hand around her cabin door and proclaimed, "This room is protected by my angels. Don't even think about coming near me!" Her finger was wagging furiously into thin air. And would you believe, for two solid weeks, while others were seeing and hearing all sorts of strange things, Mairéad saw, heard or felt nothing nad zip zilch.

Another private ghost tour had been organised just as it had been the previous year and I was so delighted that my mother was fit and well enough, in her late eighties, to walk every square inch of that ship without assistance. She looked adorable in her summer white outfit, always with a trusty cardigan in case the air conditioning was a bit too chilly. Our tour guide was an absolute character and informed us that he also performed in a drag show in his spare time. He fell in love with Mom and she thought he was the cat's meow. His energy and passion made each and every ghost story come to life. He took Mom by the hand and personally walked her down the many flights of stairs and into the engine room. I stood next to Mom as he told the tale of the maintenance man who had been severed in two when a water-tight door slammed shut on him during a routine fire drill. Mom turned to me in the middle of the talk and said it had felt like someone had put a hand on her. I was the only one standing directly next to her and I wouldn't have been able to keep a straight face if it had been me. She was totally serious and insisted that she hadn't just been caught up in the atmosphere and imagined it. When we emerged from the bottom of the ship, Mom found a bench to sit on for a little rest.

She went to put her cardigan around her shoulders, as we were now actually outside of the ship and there was a nip in the air. As she pulled the sweater around her, both of us gasped. On the sleeve of her pristine, white cardigan was a perfect, greasy black handprint. "I told you someone grabbed me!" She was more excited than alarmed. When our tour guide came over to see what all the fuss was about, he had that *"this was not part of the tour"* look on his face. He was truly dumbfounded, begging Mom to report it to the front desk, where on-going records were kept of ghostly interactions encountered by passengers. If nothing else had happened on the entire trip, Mom would have been perfectly satisfied. To this day, that cardigan has never been washed, hangs in a plastic bag in the closet and comes out whenever Mom gives a program to any of her book clubs or church groups about her time aboard the Queen Mary.

Interesting stories of the Queen Mary, you say, but what does any of it have to do with a new understanding or healing of any sort? Well, there's one more story that I hope will be of use to anyone out there who has ever dealt with a 'haunted' property. What I'm about to share isn't the be all and end all of answers to every haunted location, but for me, it created a new awareness that had never been a possibility in my mind until it was perfectly explained to me. On our second stint aboard the QM, some friends had decided to stay in the most famous cabin the ship had to offer; the Winston Churchill Suite. Churchill had spent a considerable amount of time in the 1940's aboard the 'Grey Ghost', his *mistress of the sea* and had quite an affinity for her. Passengers who had previously stayed in the Churchill Suite had reported the sudden and very strong smell of cigar smoke, extreme temperature changes, clacking and banging, in addition to a host of other paranormal activities.

One morning, during the course of my two week stay, I was sitting on the edge of my bed after taking a shower. I had leaned forward, hanging my head down to towel dry my hair. When I flipped my head back up... *there he was.* An apparition of Winston Churchill, as clear as day, was right there in front of me. To many, I'm sure it seems pretty strange, but for someone who has been talking to the spirit world all of her life, it wasn't such a big shock. I guess if there was any shock, it was *who* I was having a conversation with as opposed to *what* I was speaking to. This chat will forever be in my heart because this essence of Churchill so thoroughly explained a concept that had me completely perplexed.

Most of the time when I am communicating with those who have crossed over or even those who never lived in this realm in the first place, it is in order to pass on information that is relevant or helpful to another individual's healing or soul progression. Only in recent years have I dealt with a higher number of entities that are hanging about with the intention of lowering vibration, doing damage or attempting to temporarily disrupt a person's higher good, (ultimately for their higher purpose). I had always wondered, if a house or a property or even a person was *haunted* by one or multiple spirits did this mean that these spirits were all trapped here, unable to move into the light and carry on with their soul's evolution? Come on...Stuck? Imprisoned? All of them?

For example, it really bothered me that so many people would report seeing the little girl with the big red bow on board the Queen Mary. She had drowned in the ship's swimming pool and has been hanging around it ever since. The maintenance man who was killed during the fire drill; there have been multiple sightings of this poor guy. It really bugged me that no one with the capacity to assist these spirits in to the light had been successful in doing so, in addition to the fact that these captive souls had failed to progress and this was being capitalized on as a selling point for the ship's visitor trade.

It was Winston Churchill, or some part of his spirit, who cleared this up for me. Churchill reminded me that just as I had experienced in my own near-death event, the soul and its conscious connection to the life or lives it has experienced on Earth, lives on after the physical form expires. He explained that just as we, here on Earth, enjoy going to amusement parks, allowing our intelligent minds to take temporary leave of that which we *know* to be real, spirits who dwell in the alternate reality that is tethered to the Earth plane, enjoy contributing to or partaking in the same type of entertainment. In his earthly life as Churchill, he had a great fondness for the Queen Mary and all that she had to offer. When she was permanently docked, there had to be a way to sustain her place as a playground for visitors in search of the same thrill that she had offered in her heyday as a working vessel. Rather than a fate of deteriorating to rust and ruin, a sort of holographic adventure playground was put in place to embellish the material renovations and repairs of the magnificent floating hotel, assuring her continued success. Knowing that I speak the language of *frequency*, I was told that the vibration of expectation had everything to do with the way people would experience their time on board *Her Majesty*.

For those who entered the engine room, for example, with the anticipation that they would see, hear or feel something *out of this world*, the frequency of their expectation could trip a switch of sorts, setting in to motion a holographic series of events that would match or exceed their wildest dreams. Therefore, the girl with the bow, the maintenance man and even my friend, the jewellery thief, were projected phantasmagorias or optical illusions set up by those in spirit with a connection to the Queen Mary who had an interest in seeing her live on well in to the future. These images work on a loop, providing visual, auditory and kinaesthetic realities for those who are in search of them. It is also for this reason that my friend, Mairéad, was able to spend two weeks on the QM without seeing or hearing a single thing, while those around her were reporting the most fantastic experiences of the supernatural. She had emphatically declared what she *would not* witness; therefore her vibration did not match or set anything out of the ordinary in to motion. My mother, on the other hand, could not wait to see something mystical and her frequency of expectancy created an entirely different experience during her stay. No soul was trapped, forever doomed to wander the halls of nautical antiquity, yet anyone who was able to trip the vibration of a haunted encounter, was in for the time of their life.

This is certainly not the case in every location that reports paranormal activity, as circumstances are as varied as the people who live them. There are other reasons; ley lines, vortices, Earth bound entities and a host of other factors that can be responsible for mystical happenstances. That's a book all on its own. For me, this was a most beneficial revelation in my development as a facilitator of healing. I will always have a soft spot for the Queen Mary, as well as Winston Churchill, because of our unique encounters and the new understandings they provided. When in the business of assisting others to comprehend the intricacies of how our minds, bodies and spirits actually operate, new insights, especially those from *the other side*, are unreservedly invaluable.

When Cancer Is the Answer

The Universe does have a brilliant sense of timing, and quite often I have found myself at the receiving end of some pretty big jokes and even bigger lessons. Christmas 2008, will always be a big one in my understanding of what it means to heal. My children's father, who had left the country several years prior, had pleaded with me to let him take our girls for a few weeks. Not only did he want them for the holidays, he wanted to take them to Disney World; *The Magic Kingdom*. He had not handled our break-up very responsibly. I had been left to raise the girls without his physical, emotional or financial assistance. The healer in me wanted to let them go. They had a once or twice a year brief visit with their Dad and now had the opportunity to go somewhere very special with him. I thought the chance to create some happy memories would be good for them all. The bitter and betrayed shadow side of me wanted nothing more than to tell him where he could go...and it 'twernt' to Florida!

"You're going to Disney, girls!" I announced, amidst squeals of delight.

Right decision? Is there such a thing? I chose what I thought was the path of least resistance; a trip to Disney in Orlando, Florida for the girls while I stayed with my Auntie Joyce, in nearby DeLand. I would get to see my oldest brother and a healthy portion of my extended family. The deal also included a trip home to Virginia to see my parents; a win win situation all the way around, or so I thought. What I didn't realise at the time, was that the tiny raw spot in my heart that I had long since plastered over with positive affirmations, laughter and numerous healing sessions, was still, in fact, just a little too raw.

Disney at Christmas is simply spectacular. I recommend the experience to children of all ages. Trees full of sparkling baubles, princesses in red velvet gowns, snow on Main Street America after a day in the blazing hot sun; it's every kid's dream. The enchanted kingdom left my daughters full of wonder and delight, something I felt they deserved after a very tough couple of years.

Me? I was strong and I knew I could handle whatever came my way. Reality? I watched my children bask in the love of both of their parents, simultaneously, as I met them for a day with Mickey Mouse and friends. This was something they were too young to remember when it happened last. I was treading on very dangerous ground. Suddenly, all of my strength, my resolve to live my life in my own best interest, was beginning to succumb to the magic of Disney; a fantasy world of happy endings, where adversity was always overcome by true love. For a brief moment, I allowed myself to consider the possibility, despite all that had gone down with my former partner in the past; a family unit, a loving mother and father putting their own differences aside to create a stable home for their children. I felt the love... that is, until the rage set in.

Who did he think he was? What was I thinking? I had raised those girls, I had been there for every cough and cold, every scraped knee, every dance recital, every visit from the tooth fairy, Every Everything! He had run. I had supported those children on my own. How could I have agreed to let him swan in and take the girls to the most fantastic place on Earth? It should have been me! It should have been me...That tiny little raw spot had festered into a putrefied, open wound. *I sooo thought I was past this.*

When we said our goodbyes, I ran for my life, all the while, wiping the girls' tears as they left their Dad behind, not knowing when they might see him again. I was never so relieved to reach the safety of my childhood home in Virginia. Mom and Dad were delighted to see their Irish grand-babies and I had never been so happy to see my parents. I needed my own Mommy. I was safe for the time being...from me, and from my foolish heart.

The girls and I returned to Ireland, ready to start 2009 with a bang. It was not just any bang. It was a Big Bang. I found myself in a parallel existence. Was it 2009 or 1993? Standing in the shower, a routine wash, not an exam, inadvertently revealed a familiar feeling. This time, I wasn't twenty-two, in a marriage to my best friend that was destined not to last. I was a month shy of forty, and had just returned from a blast to the past with the girls' father that was so fraught with emotion, I had, for the second time in my life, developed a breast tumour.

A trip to the hospital in Galway disclosed what I already knew. The response from this surgeon was also the same as it had been in Charleston, South Carolina nearly twenty years earlier, when I had been given the same diagnosis for the first time.

"Give me three weeks." I insisted.

"That's not a good idea."

"I just needed confirmation that my disgust with my recent choices have now manifested physically."

(I was undeniably certain that a smattering of victim mentality had slipped under my radar.)

"That's very forward thinking, but I don't think you should neglect proper medical attention just to prove a point." My doctor offered. "We may be able to surgically remove it all without having to use ra..."

"Ah, ah ah... Don't even say the words! I did this to myself, I will fix this myself." I refused to give it any further energy.

"I'm scheduling you for immediate...

"I'll see you for a check-up before a month is up. If my way hasn't worked, then we'll talk about your proposed solution." I spoke emphatically.

She nodded, knowing there was absolutely no use trying to change my mind.

I left the clinic, drove to a beach on the Atlantic Coast road, sat by the water and cried. I didn't cry in fear of her diagnosis, I had already known what that would be. I didn't cry because I was unsure of my future. That, too, I knew was secured. I cried to allow myself to be angry. I was, after all, human. An unusual specimen, to say the least, but I was human. I had missed the mark. I had stepped out of character, away from all that I had learned from facilitating healings, and had created the perfect circumstances for my emotions to make me sick.

Only a few weeks earlier, I had allowed the girls to go to Disney with their father, yet I had made one lethal error. It wasn't with unconditional love that I had sent them on their way. I thought that it was best for them to develop happy, all be they brief memories, with their long-distance Daddy, *regardless of my feelings*. Had I done this with no emotional angst or attachments, the outcome most likely would have been very different. It certainly was no coincidence. I had just become a very common statistic, and I knew better. I've never yet met a breast tumour that didn't involve over-nurturing on some level, regardless of whether physical, chemical or emotional influences had been the initial catalyst.

The healer began to heal that afternoon on the shores of the Atlantic. I reflected on the recent events, shook hands with the anger, the betrayal of my feelings, not by my old flame, but by me. No one had forced me to do anything. It certainly wasn't his fault. I had made the ultimate decision to allow the girls time with their absentee father. Under an overcast, Irish sky, the islands in the distance seemed so mysterious and wise; the perfect backdrop for self-discovery. I expressed my thanks for the experience of being human and mapped out a plan. As with all things that I chalk up to experience, I knew that this, too, would find a perfect place in the annals of my history and that I would use it someday to help anyone with ears to hear it.

A focused intent, a diet of raw foods and two and a half bottles of home-made Cancer Tea would complete the task at hand. With each day that passed, my confidence grew, my tumour shrank and the time returned that I would see the surgeon for my follow-up appointment in Galway.

"Remarkable." All she could do was shake her head.

"I thought you'd say that. Will I tell how I did it?"

She smiled as I shared my insights and I knew that our worlds were so close, yet so far away. To accept my approach to healing would explode the very foundations upon which her belief systems *and her career* had been built. I also knew this would never happen to me again.

"I'll see you in six months for a check-up."

"Thanks for the offer, but it's not necessary. I promise I'll always keep tabs on the situation, but I've checked this box off for the last time."

It wouldn't be long before the opportunity to use this experience would walk through my own office door.

An exhausted mother of three had been advised to come to me for a session, following her diagnosis of advanced breast cancer. Younger than me, her haggard appearance suggested a real struggle in her personal life which had completely worn her out. She lay on the table, and I placed my hand over her solar plexus, the seat of her personal identity, her value and worth as an individual. It was as if I had put my hand in a vacuum.

"Why do you think you have Cancer?" I got straight to the point, knowing what her answer would be.

"Excuse me?" *Why?* Is that what you said? I just got it. It just got me."

"Ah, so you are a victim of Cancer, is that correct?"

"You make it sound like... you make it sound like I had some kind of control over whether I got it or not. Who in the world would do this to themselves?" Her voice trembled not with fear, but with temper.

It was clear that she was beginning to think she had made a terrible mistake coming to me. That is, until I went all psychic on her.

"Let me get the story straight. How long have you had Cancer?"

"One year."

"And it's about a year and a half since you found out about your husband's affair, is that right?"

She shot bolt upright on the table and cried out,

"Do you know him?!?!" I chuckled and shook my head no.

You see, this is where the intuitive stuff comes in handy. A little shock value when trying to prove a point can create quite an impact.

She lay back down and through tears asked how I could have possibly known about her husband's infidelity. I explained to her that her energy body told me. I touched her, 'read' her recent history pertaining to the illness and helped her to connect the dots. I'm a dot connector.

"I don't understand" she sobbed.

"You will. I promise. Let's see if there is a possibility, a tiny, remote chance, that Cancer has in anyway improved your life."

Now she knew I was nuts, but she played along anyway.

"Since you found out about the Cancer, how has life changed for you at home?"

"It's been horrible. I'm exhausted, the treatment has kept it from getting worse but I haven't gotten any better."

"So, you're a fence-sitter."

"A what?" She was getting slightly agitated again.

Just how I wanted her.

"A fence-sitter; no better, no worse." I explained.

"I suppose, if you put it like that, yes."

"I want to know how your life has changed for the better." With that, she kept silent.

"How on earth do you cope at home now, with the sickness and the exhaustion, while your husband is out having an affair?" I had carefully posed my question with a slight hint of sarcasm.

"Oh, I see! No, no, no... That all stopped right after I was diagnosed. He's been as good as gold to me! There is no time, no way; he has to be home to take care of the children, to take me to my appointments, to cook the dinners, to... Oh.My.God."

I smiled. There is nothing more gratifying than the moment the proverbial light bulb goes 'CLICK'!

"Sooo", I inflected melodically.

"Life has changed a whole lot since you 'got' this Cancer. It sounds like the family unit was forced to work together again... *just the way you wanted it to.*"

"Oh, my God! Are you saying I created this in order to get my husband back?"

"What I am saying, is that no disease happens without just cause. You are not a victim. Did you confront your husband when you found out about the affair?"

"No, I was too afraid. I was petrified of what he might say; that he might just walk away. Most of all, I was terrified of what it would do to our children."

(Can we say...over-nurturing?)

"Could you entertain the possibility that in place of dealing with your problems with your husband, you created a more 'comfortable', way to change the scenario?"

"Comfortable?? You're kidding, right? I'm dying, here! Seriously, I'm stage four, remember?"

"I mean comfortable in the sense that you didn't have to directly confront your husband, but through illness you accomplished the ultimate result, as in, the end of his affair."

"Do I have that kind of power?" She asked, sincerely.

"You do, and the good news is that same power can get you off that freakin' fence and heal this Cancer. I've seen your soul plan; you totally have the choice to change this. You do not have to die this way."

In the middle of it all, she began to fidget.

"What are you doing with your hands? My boob feels really hot."
The entire time we had been speaking, I had been holding my left hand directly over the affected breast with my right hand stuck firmly to her solar plexus, the seat of her own self-worth.

"I've done my bit. This is in your hands now, my dear. Make a choice."

"Now?"

"Can you think of a better time? What's it going to be?" I asked, in earnest.

"I choose me. I choose life." Tears streamed down her cheeks.

A few weeks had passed, when guess who came a callin'? That's right...the husband. His wife's improvement had been dramatic and rapid. So much so, that it had scared the living daylights out of him when she finally chose to deal with the real issue and he was forced to truly own up to his affair. I had to gently remind him as he stammered through his introduction, that I was not his priest and this was not confession. He did not owe me an explanation. If he needed guidance that was one thing, but I think what he really wanted to know was *how* I knew about the affair.
He wasn't buying the whole 'I read it in her energy field' thing, but it wasn't too long before he was on the flat of his back, connecting his own dots... *and a few home truths*. The greatest gift I could give to him was the understanding that he was not the cause, but the catalyst of his wife's experience. He was genuinely guilt-ridden, and as we know, that's a fast train to nowhere nice.

By the end of our session, I am fairly confident that he had a better understanding as to how his actions had created a clear cut reaction that ultimately taught his wife that she is master of her own fate. My advice to him? Release the guilt, embrace the gift of participation in such a monumental event and get on with it. I didn't expect for him fully understand the idea that on a soul level he had actually agreed to betray his wife in order for her to step up and consider herself worthy of love. Because of his actions, she now owned the concept of self-acceptance. But somehow, I think some part of him actually got it.

To this day, they continue to experience their life adventures as husband and wife, and she is Cancer free. How long did it take? About three and a half weeks.

I want to make something perfectly clear. I do not believe that in all cases an illness is created because of one specific event. Usually it's quite the opposite. I have spent a lifetime educating myself about mind-sets. I was at a place within my own experiences that allowed me to manifest and rid myself of a malady in a short space of time. I've also been studying these concepts, watching them in action in other people's lives for years.

For many people that I work with, the detrimental mind-set or habitual behavioural patterns that they have carried throughout their *entire* life experience, eventuate into a disease process. You don't smoke one cigarette and get cancer, nor does one fleeting negative thought result in a stress-induced ailment. The story above is a classic example. The fact that this woman developed breast cancer shortly after finding out about her husband's affair was a 'straw that broke the camel's back' scenario. She had spent a lifetime in fear of upsetting the apple cart, petrified that if she spoke her mind or stood up for herself, the outcome would be worse than the offence. It finally came to a head with her husband's affair.

Most people, believe it or not, are not spiritually disciplined enough to manifest and heal overnight. Like I said before, disciplined or not, in my case, I had missed the mark. I knew better, and did it anyway; I'm aware...but most certainly not immune to a friendly reminder that I must always keep a close watch on my own thoughts and behaviours. The human body truly is an incredible system of checks and balances, allowing us to manifest the exact emotional or physical states that will best support our individual missions while here on Earth.

Indigo is a Shade of Blue

I had the great pleasure of working with a young man who was about to discover that there was a method to what he, himself, considered to be madness. Having self-harmed and botched up a suicide attempt, resulting in permanent damage to his hand, after years of anguish and self-doubt, he knew that it was time to start asking some different questions. From the moment he walked through the door, I knew that I was in the presence of greatness.

Nancy Ann Tappe, PhD., counsellor, metaphysician, and author of "Understanding Your Life through Color", is widely accredited for first coining a term that to those in 'the business', is now commonplace. The first book dedicated solely to the topic of 'Indigo Children', was written by Lee Carroll and Jan Tober in 1999. "The Indigo Children; The New Kids Have Arrived" was a ground-breaking work that used first-hand accounts from accredited teachers, children's workers and other professionals to highlight the fact that an astounding number of children that came into this world at the later end of the 20th century, displayed characteristics and skills far beyond those that had previously been apparent in the 'average' child. Call them what you will, these extraordinary individuals are on a mission and we've never experienced anything like these new kids in recent global memory, if ever. No label, mainstream or metaphysical, would ever be able to box these amazing souls into anything resembling the status quo.

For the most part, those who tend to be categorized as Indigo are actually children who display a wide range of characteristics from being highly sensitive and perceptive, to misunderstood and misdiagnosed as hyperactive, learning disabled on the autism spectrum or unable to adjust to mainstream forms of education. They are fiery and passionate and if steered in the right direction, have the capacity to create unlimited change. They are recognised by a resistance to a lack of integrity. They cannot be lied to and detest the idea that just because an adult wants them to behave in a way that is more manageable, that they must conform.

These souls are here to collapse our out-dated archetypes, to challenge the very systems that have left us in a complete state of dishonour. If this passion is not focused or channelled in a positive forward direction, some of the 'new kids' have the potential to go within, questioning their decision to come into a world that is so completely screwed up. They can become aggressive, harming themselves and others out of sheer despair for the ignorance and greed displayed by those who they feel have been irresponsible with life. Recognised and supported for their mission to make drastic changes in the thought processes of the world at large, these unique personalities have the potential to become activists, inventors and major contributors to a more productive global community. With a temperament that can be interpreted as argumentative or unruly, these 'new kids' can make those who are conformists, extremely uncomfortable with their incessant need to know WHY? Sweeping problems under the carpet or being forced to remain quiet and not question authority are the very things that drive these people either to distraction or into the forefront of creativity and invention.

One of the world's foremost authorities on the subject of near-death, American researcher, PMH Atwater, has recently written "A Manual for Developing Humans". Apart from being the only book of its kind and literally channelled from 'out of this world', the manual gives a perfect explanation of these 'new kids', those who have worn labels from every available diagnosis on the Autism spectrum to the colour of Indigo. Pay Amazon a little visit and treat yourself to this paradigm-shifting material. Atwater explains these astonishing children and the reason they are here with the precision and eloquence they deserve.

When Sean MacAoide landed on my table, there was far more than the signature iridescent indigo blue swirling around in his auric field. There was an air of hopefulness in his desperation, that led me to believe that he wanted nothing more than for someone to understand who and what he really was. The session was powerful for both of us. I revisited my personal commitment to help people exactly like him to tap in to their divinity. He, in turn, realised that he was not alone. Through self-inflicted harm, this man had danced with death and his devil, inside. It was then that I took the opportunity to give him a different perspective on the subject.

I have worked with so many people who have attempted self-annihilation; some, who were still actively contemplating the option at the time of our meeting. There are those who may think that my approach is risky, and that anyone with suicidal tendencies should be handled with velvet gloves. I choose to tell them like it was told to me when I was hovering between being alive and dead at the time of my car accident, being prepared for a life of service to my fellow human beings. Being honest, I can report that I have never lost a single one of them to suicide due to overwhelm. Overwhelm attempts can be overcome; a soul plan suicide can rarely be changed.

Once outside the confines of religion or judgement, when a person connects with the idea that suicide is one of any number of ways in which a soul can depart from this world, it begins to lose its seductive appeal. If the soul plan is such that a spirit decides before incarnation that it will leave via suicide in order to provide a maximum growth experience for the souls with whom it interacts while on Earth, then the consequences are the very same as those experienced by the individual who dies from illness, a tragic accident, old age, etc. The exit from the body starts the very same way, with an increase in the vibration of the auric or energy field which looks a lot like a beautiful fireworks display. This can begin days, weeks or months prior to the actual exit. The soul then returns to a higher vibration where it reunites with other members of its soul group. There is a cleansing, a removal of the veil of forgetfulness that allows the spirit to fully integrate the lessons of that human experience, and a return to the *knowing* that we are pure energy and light. Heaven? No. It's the space between lives as the soul continues to incarnate in the Earth plane or prepares to move on to another phase of corporeal or etheric existence. The other side of this life is infinitely dimensional. Heaven is the voyage, the feeling, the frequency of light; not a destination.

Read that last line again…

There are also occasions when it *is not* on a soul's plan to die via suicide. Life and free will may have created a series of events that eventually become too overpowering, leaving the individual feeling so completely isolated, so hopeless, that ending it all seems the only way to make the hurting stop. If the suicide by overwhelm is carried through, once again, there is the fireworks display as the soul prepares to leave; there is the exit, the cleansing, a moment of realisation like "Aww, man! I can't believe I forgot!", then a return to the loving embrace of the soul group. *That's it.*

There is no punishment, no retribution, no condemnation from a vengeful God, only the keen awareness that this soul can return again, recreate a series of circumstances that will cause them to re-visit the choice, with the opportunity to handle things differently. They may then complete the full set of tasks laid out by non-other than… themselves. It won't be in the same body, with exactly the same characters, characteristics or location. It could be despair in a recession in Dublin rather than abuse as a child in Johannesburg; drug addiction in Sydney, or bullying in St. Augustine. The situation won't be the same, but the *feeling* that goes with it will be identical. It always has been and forever will be, all about the frequency or feeling of an experience.

Sean MacAoide now had the urge to connect with other 'new kids' on the block. He knew that in his lack of purpose he had found his plan. A gifted poet, he shared with me a few verses that I think epitomize the classic 'new kid' life form. Deep, introspective and painful expressions followed by a fresh outlook on the very reason he had chosen the life that he had so desperately wanted to leave behind. I marvel at his talent for expression and am so blessed to call him my friend.

As an Indigo I get these thoughts rushing through my head
Keeping me up late at night, when I should be in bed.
I've seen life's horrors and what they've done to me
Locked away as a child, I only wanted to flee.
Not knowing how to control my head, these thoughts pushing through
Looking back as an adult, if only then I knew.
What I have is a gift that God sent from above
At times it's hard to see it, when your life is lacking love.
If only someone would reach to me and try to understand
I am not a monster, but a misunderstood man.
For all I want in the world is for people to be kind
And not try and mould me and see things from their mind.
For my mind is racing, and on and on it goes
I got rid of negativity and now I let it flow.
None of us are different, we all bleed the same
So please stop looking at me as if I was to blame.
There is so much I can offer, if only you let me in
I'm not trying to hurt you or even cause you sin.
Let me tell you that I love you and I hope you understand
With these thoughts rushing, I need love to become a man.
When I'm there I'll show you a brighter story to be told
I'll take away the darkness and let the colours unfold.
For I felt like an alien trapped in human skin
But now you see me shining and flowing from within.
It took some time to get here, the journey sometimes bold
But now I see Love through my eyes
I'll let my life unfold.

-Sean MacAoide

Sean now spends his free time away from his very busy and successful business with the beautiful woman who accepts *all of him*. His wife is a special breed, not always completely able to understand where her husband's mind takes him, but perfectly willing to trust that he must follow his chosen path. Theirs is a groovy kind of love, and I feel so fortunate to have had the experience to witness the enigmatic nature of their relationship, up close and personal. Sean also shares his musings with others who are walking a similar path, through an internet society chat room.

He has found that his particular 'shade of blue' is as diverse as the colours of the rainbow. I know, for fact, that he is touching lives by sharing his own self- discoveries. It's what he came here to do. He has also realised something that all who work for the light have come to know. We are ushering in a new generation of higher vibration beings who are so intuitive; they no longer need the tragic experiences. These sentient beings are choosing families who can provide the emotions of the tragic, without having to experience the actual trauma. I hound Sean every time I see him to write a book of life through a 'new kid's' eyes. Some day…

We're all going to expire, eventually. We can eat, drink or stress ourselves to death over a long period of time, we can die of old age, we can be murdered or killed in an accident or we can take our own lives in an instant. The judgements around what we consider an acceptable or honourable death are man-made. I have found that in all but one case that I can recall, every potential suicide that has landed on my doorstep, was innately looking for an intervention. I have worked with many families and friends who have lost someone to a soul plan suicide, but rarely do they seek help or attention before taking their leave. The one I met who was *not* seeking assistance was looking for a peaceful transition as she entered what she knew, with all of her heart, was her chosen way out. This was her soul's plan. I have known many families who have lost someone dear because of a soul plan suicide and felt very honoured that I had the opportunity to get a first-hand account of another human's *knowing* of this form of exit.

This lovely lady's advancing terminal illness and subsequent death by suicide was monumental in the lives of those who loved her. She was not looking for me to talk her out of it or to tell her what I knew about life and death. *She gifted me* with the opportunity to gain a deeper understanding through a very candid dialogue of what a suicide by soul plan looked like on this side of life. The difference is unmistakable. She genuinely remembered the agreement she had made with members of her soul group to exit by her own hand, in turn leaving them with the immense learning that could be obtained by dealing with death by suicide. She was offering *her people* the chance to get sucked up in the drama of guilt, anger and rage, or in turn, the opportunity to recognise that we are not responsible for the life paths or decisions of others...ever. We can influence, give guidance and direction, but ultimately we cannot live the life or control the circumstances of death for another, though many amongst us will die trying. For her courage to share this insight with me, knowing that I would in turn share it with you, I am deeply grateful.

While on the subject of the 'new kids', it is important to acknowledge that there are many valiant souls that chose to incarnate to assist these 'new kids' and others on their mission to change the world. They come in the form of parents, teachers, care workers and special friends, here to accept, listen and guide those who will escort us into a new era in the history of humanity.

I love this topic, because while I carry and understand so many of the characteristics of these highly intuitive and sensitive types of children, I also chose to parent a couple of them. Talk about in your face! With my two, both equally gifted in the psychic sense, their personalities and the way they learn, express and interact with others, is as if they are literally from two different planets.

Jemma, my eldest, is an empathic, sensitive soul; I can't walk with her through the streets of Dublin without watching her become an emotional basket case when she approaches someone who is homeless. It enrages her and fills her with an inconsolable sadness. Jada, on the other hand, will walk up to someone who is homeless, chat to them and then drop a coin in the cup. Jemma will try to give them my entire wallet, unable to speak through her genuine sobs. Jemma hates that our world would allow such atrocity. Jada, on the other hand, is wildly inquisitive about the choices they have made, and doesn't appear to harbour the deep emotion about why they are in the state that they are in. It's as if she just trusts that they *know* what they are doing on a soul level. Neither is wrong. They represent two entirely different types of champion, working towards the same goal. One is a bulldozer, the other a street cleaner. I'm in awe of them both.

When Teacher Becomes Student

Whenever an individual comes to me for a session, unless there is a pressing issue that I feel needs to be further investigated, I always leave the decision to return for a follow-up visit up to them. For many, once is all it takes. There are some who love the great unknown, the idea of what else can be unravelled from the shadows of their mind. These are the dear souls I will see periodically. There are also a few who simply float on air after being bathed in the healing Solfeggio frequencies, the tools I often use to recalibrate and balance energetic vibrations. For these individuals, a session with me is their equivalent of going off for a pampering spa day to soothe the body; in my office, they come to soothe the soul. To each his own, and as I tell everyone who crosses my threshold, there simply are no rules within the confines of my healing room. All are welcome, be it once or as many times as they choose.

One of the most fortunate relationships I have ever been blessed with is a kind-hearted, deeply spiritual woman named Sarah Jane. Several decades my senior, through the honour of assisting in her healing process, she has become one of my most powerful instructors and a most treasured friend. She is a perfect example of someone who incarnated into the old world mind-set with a new world mentality. Teaching within the Catholic school system, Sarah Jane was the perfect candidate to bridge the gap between church doctrine and spiritualism. I began working with Sarah Jane in early 2006. So much took place during our sessions over the years that I decided to wait until now to introduce her story. There are so many who come for healing who get what they need in one visit. A few use our time together as regular maintenance for the soul. Neither one is more valid than the other. I will share Sarah Jane's words first. I will then fill you in on one of the most astonishing sessions I have ever facilitated.

> *My earliest memories are of life in rural Ireland. Endless summer days playing on the farm, and dark, winter nights, the wind whistling outside. Those were wet, cold and dreary days. I was born in the early 1940's, brought up in a strict Catholic family. Everyone attended Mass, sacraments and missions. It was the accepted way of life. The priest was revered and feared. He was a man with authority. Our priest was kind, caring, genial and much loved by all.*

> *I read extensively and came to a knowledge of cultural difference. During my college years and adult studies, I had many encounters that challenged my view of the world. I questioned my religious beliefs and came to a deeper understanding of faith and life. My mind opened to other religions, races, cultural diversities and also to an appreciation of my own journey. My faith and upbringing colours my perspective. I am enriched by the beliefs and customs of other people.*

> *In the autumn of my life, I had the opportunity to make my inward journey to look back over the years to reflect, pray, think and most of all, to draw my experiences together. At this time, I was ill. For the first time, death seemed a reality. I wasn't prepared to embrace it just then.*

> *I met Mary Helen; a breath of fresh air. She blew my mind! It was an amazing experience when she took me on a journey that is difficult to describe. Her ideas, her world, her experiences were beyond my comprehension. I spent two years in this wonderful space, integrating my life. It was like turning the pages of a book and my story unfolded, picture by picture. My dreams led to places unknown, to times long forgotten, to emotions suppressed and never expressed.*

> *I reflected and let go of my baggage; the hurts, real and imaginary. My vision of the world expanded and my place in the Universe became clearer.Life is an expression of*

who we are; the greatness of the human spirit. Religion and Christianity are core elements of my life. I am in no way less Christian because of my experience. I am whole, integrated and I have a more rounded view of my purpose in life and the possibilities ahead.

My journey was painful and at times, disconcerting. I took all of the time I needed to allow the new experiences to permeate my thought process.

Communicating with people who have passed on, as well as reincarnation, are now concepts that I am open to as a possibility. I am respectful of the views of others. Mary Helen's perspectives on life are beyond my wildest imagination. I have made a journey with her which has led me to openness and acceptance of difference. My life is richer, with endless possibilities in my winter years.

Each day is a new beginning. I believe in the value of life and in the contribution we make to society. The message in Christianity and countless other religions, that we will meet our loved ones again, is very real. It has already happened to me.

To the future with Hope.
Sarah Jane

Sarah Jane is kind with her words, but the truth be told, she has been more dedicated to accountability and change in her own life than almost any other person I have worked with...ever. Because of her tenacity and her deep longing to integrate and then release her past experiences, Sarah Jane was given a most unexpected and overwhelming gift from beyond.

It was a crisp, autumn evening. The office was quiet, and Sarah Jane and I were in my new healing room for the first time. We had previously conducted all of our sessions in the physical therapy room, where I had been holding court for the last few years. Surrounded by soothing browns, creams and turquoise, we christened this new space together. As usual, she was so disciplined in her regiment of giving herself permission to let go, she quickly drifted in to a relaxed, meditative zone where whatever was going to happen, could happen.

Only minutes in to our adventure, a former student of hers made his introduction. He identified himself by the nickname he had given to Sarah Jane when he was a rowdy pupil in her classroom, many moons ago. She remembered him and the cheeky moniker very well. Sarah Jane's immediate response was one of sadness, as she didn't even realise that he had passed away. But this was soon replaced with laughter, as he reminded her of some of his off-colour antics while under her tutelage. Before she even had a chance to digest the unexpected appearance of this playful apparition, in wafted another. This time, it was a female. She described how things for her had been quite dreadful at home as a youngster. The one constant she had been able to count on during that dark time in her life was Sarah Jane. My eyes welled up with tears right along with Sarah Jane's, as this spirit shared the impact that her former teacher had made on her life. Sarah Jane had never realised...

One by one, my small healing room was now filling up with energies that were eager to shower Sarah Jane with positive affirmations about her life's work. It had nothing to do with religion or the subject matter that she had taught. These former human beings were letting Sarah Jane know that it was SHE who had made a categorical difference in their lives. Overcome by the palpable love that was literally expanding our cosy space, Sarah Jane and I were both moved beyond words. I don't get emotional too often in these sessions, but on this day, my heart would have been made of stone if I hadn't. We laughed, sobbed, she shouted thank you at the ceiling, and we blubbered our way through an entire box of tissues before it was all over.

In all of my days, I have never seen anything quite like it. What an absolute testimony to a life of service. If ever she had questioned her chosen path and the stringent parameters it had required, she had been shown beyond a shadow of a doubt that her choices had mattered. Not only to her, but to the members of a very grateful group that represented only a fraction of the lives that she had touched. Understanding the massive impact she had made on her student's lives became the foundation of her personal healing process.

Nun Sense

Una was not the first nun I had come across in my sessions. A surprisingly large number of Sisters, Brothers and Fathers have landed on my table over the years, in search of direction. Nearly twice my age, Una was a breath of fresh air with her open mind, unbelievable accounts of life in service to the church, and her willingness to continue her education as a student of life.

Una describes herself in the springtime of her youth as a roamer and wanderer. She was always contemplating the meaning of life. The 'accepted' norm for a young girl to grow up, get married and raise a family just never appealed to her. She recalls that she was always stuck in a book, looking for adventure, *looking for God*. At the age of sixteen, the decision for her was black and white. Rather than succumb to boredom on a life path that most girls her age seemed to be choosing, Una made the decision to become a nun.

It was never so much about the religion for her. The thrill of discovering new cultures, different languages, seeing the world from outside of Ireland's eye was what captured her heart. She spent time in Tunisia, then Egypt, experiencing dirt poverty at a level she had only read about at home. Her travels eventually landed her in Suez, where she was sent to work in the Suez Canal Dispensary.

On the night that the canal was nationalised in July of 1956, the world, *and a few unsuspecting nuns* were all taken by surprise. There was loud banging at the door of the convent where Una and her sisters were residing. Una looked out over the balcony only to see the Egyptian army below in their heavily armoured vehicles. The sisters refused to open the doors. In an alarming act of violence, the army transports smashed through the entrance of the convent. Politics ensued and the French sisters who were housed in the convent were taken captive, subjected to unspeakable crimes. Because of the passports they held, a terrified Una and a Belgian sister were left behind. The two young women eventually escaped and were soon evacuated to Cairo. Something as simple as their nationalities had saved Una and her Belgian friend from the unthinkable fates that befell their other sisters in the convent.

"What in the world did the church do when they heard about the incident?" I was wildly enthralled by this first-hand account of history in the Suez.

Una chuckled slightly, rolled her eyes, and then stunned me with her response.

"They scolded and reprimanded us for abandoning our post."

I couldn't believe my ears.

My time with Una continues to be a learning process for us both. Her gift to me is in the sharing of life adventures that one could only read about in thriller novels. To her, I have given a space to integrate those experiences in to a life review on this side of the veil. As she settles in to her winter years, Una is determined to gather as much information and perspective on different views of spirituality as time will allow. While so many her age are resting in their rockers, Una continues to expand her mind and broaden her horizons, in attempts to better know her true self and the real meaning behind the life that she chose. Because she spent her life in service to the Catholic church, a great deal of Una's healing comes from focusing on the great good that she did while working as a nun. So many of her beliefs were turned on their ear when 'real life' forced Una to attempt to apply Catholic dogma where dogma simply wouldn't do. Guilt is one of the hottest topics when I'm working with my religious folks. Believe it or not, it's generally a guilt that was acquired after serving the church's interpretation of 'the Lord's work'.

I live in a country where the predominant religion is one that does not allow those who have been called to service of the church, to express love and intimacy of a romantic nature. I have always found this perplexing. I know that those who have made the choice also had the choice not to make it. But in speaking to many who have remained in service and equally as many who decided to walk away, this has been an underlying issue that has created a lot of personal turmoil for some very decent people. A lot of young women and men took vows at an age when they had yet to fathom the possibility of knowing love on an intimate level, through sheer lack of life experience.

I have facilitated many sessions with religious souls who lived in agony, when the natural spark of passion ignited, and due to their commitments, they were left heart-broken, feeling torn between their love of God and the love of one of God's people. The guilt and shame that this brought up for those who felt like their own human feelings had betrayed them is immense. But then again, these are the same people who adhere to an admission of 'grievous fault' via their prayers and recitations on a daily basis. It's not exactly a framework for building a sense of self-worth and value. The physical ramifications of these vows most often surface in the organs of the second chakra; the ovaries, uterus and colon for the women and the prostate and colon for the men. Suppression of natural urges without a rock-solid understanding of the depth of the commitment will inevitably manifest as a physical symptom in many of these individuals.

There are certainly those with whom I have worked who were perfectly content to have given up the right to experience the type of love found within a romantic relationship in place of a life of service to the church. But inevitably, these folks had issues in other areas where they were left wanting, unable to express aspects of their natural curiosities because of their job description, such as the concept that a soul could cohesively design the life path it is about to embark on; that it was not born of sin into a life where it would spend its days seeking forgiveness for choosing to be human. I suppose what has always bothered me is the implication that it was God who decreed or imposed these regulations. I can tell you that I have yet to meet more than handfuls who have not sincerely struggled with many of the laws put in place by the church that they serve. I also have rarely met any who have not on some level, stepped outside of these regulations and then flogged themselves for not upholding the 'word of God'. While I get the big picture, seeing the role that the church has played in bringing the opportunity for introspection, I can't help but wish for the day that this type of lesson is deemed no longer necessary.

I see people dedicate themselves to systems of belief, struggling to force the dynamic expression of their lives into a very narrow set of parameters set before them by their families, communities and educational backgrounds; however, I find great hope in people like my friend, Una. While realising that regret is futile, she focuses on the many positive contributions that working for an organised religion allowed her to make in the lives of others. In one of the most profound statements I have ever heard, she once said in front of an entire room full of people at one of my workshops,

"I'm just glad I have lived long enough to discover MY truth."

Enticing Entities

Erik was managing director of a prosperous corporation in the Netherlands. Easy on the eyes, with an athletic physique and a head full of blonde hair, perfectly bleached from plenty of quality sun-time; it was obvious that this good-natured businessman had managed to find the balance between his job, having fun and taking excellent care of himself. An avid outdoorsman, his monumental success at work meant that he was regularly able to partake in the sporting activities that 'recharged his batteries'. He was financially at the top of his game, had a deep passion for his career, had the means to indulge in the hobbies that he loved so much *and* was a loving father to a beautiful little girl. Although he was no longer involved with the mother of his child, their relationship was one of deep respect and mutual understanding that the well-being of their child always came first. Their co-parenting method far surpassed the amicable feelings that most ex-spouses or partners could only aspire to achieve. *Why in the world did this man need to see me?*

Something highly unusual was happening in Erik's otherwise perfect world. The man who seemed to have it all would regularly awaken, only to find himself curled up in a ball on his office floor, sometimes with up to four or five hours having passed. He would have no recollection of how he got there or what happened during the 'black out' time. He was temporarily consumed with a crippling fatigue following each episode. My first question was obvious. Had he been checked for irregularities in brain activity such as seizures or maybe possible heart issues? Extensive medical tests, including MRI's, CT scans and blood work revealed that his inner health was a mirror reflection of his impeccable external appearance and had left the experts completely stymied.

A friend of Erik's and previous patient of mine had given him my name. We were able to meet up shortly after, when both of us happened to be travelling to the U.K. the same weekend. At this stage, he was willing to explore any avenue that might shed some light on his bizarre black outs. It's a good thing that I'm not easily spooked, because within minutes of being on my table, no Hollywood horror movie could hold a candle to what I was about to witness.

Erik had relaxed to the point where he was almost asleep. I was standing at his feet, contemplating my approach to unlocking his body's secrets, when he began to hiss. *He* began to hiss is not really accurate, as it was quite apparent that the incredibly garish snake-like sound, was coming *out of him* but not *created by him*. His head began to thrash from side to side when he suddenly shot bolt upright and proceeded to reel off a string of obscenities that would make a hardened sailor blush. His eyes were wild and glazed over. And if this had actually been a horror film in the making, this is the point at which a sweaty, petrified priest would be shouting out biblical scripture while shoving a crucifix into the face of some demonically possessed kid whose head was spinning as he spit up green pea soup.

Erik's body flopped back on to the table, thumping and grinding gnashed teeth when *it* happened. The body levitated a good six inches off the table and slammed back down, over and over again. That's right, I said levitated, as in lifted off and actually hovered over the table. Any sane individual would probably have run for their life, realising that they were in the presence of darkness. Me?

I began to laugh. Disappointed that no one else was there to share in this spectacle, I stood my ground and held fast to the knowledge that I do not recognise, give power or creed to anything that is not of the highest good. Don't get me wrong, I know evil exists, and I know that darkness can wreak havoc on unsuspecting innocents, but as for me and my house…well, we serve the Light. The more Erik's nasty little entity thrashed his poor body about, the firmer I stood in Love. When dealing with disorganised, low vibration energies it is crucial never to bring fear into the equation. With each foul word, I countered with love, with every hiss, I referred to the light and eventually, I watched a puffy ball of smoky energy exit from Erik's solar plexus. Although no longer in his body, it was still hanging out in the room. I immediately picked up my phone and rang a dear friend in America for assistance. This healer has a gift of escorting lost or random beings, entities and attachments back home to the light. My ego would never prevent me from ensuring that a job is done, and done properly. The person's well-being is my first priority, not the need to take credit for any act of healing that ultimately belongs to the Highest Power. Healing is a team sport as far as I'm concerned.

Back on the table, Erik was soaked in sweat but his energy had definitely shifted. Aware that something had happened but not sure what, he appeared to be none the wiser as to the circus act his body had just performed while this entity was exiting his energy field.

When I explained to Erik that he had a very disagreeable little entity attachment, he immediately wanted to know if this 'thing' had been the cause of his mysterious black outs. Only time would tell.

Why him? Why can two people be exposed to the same virus and one gets ill while the other does not? If the circumstances are just right in the host body, a virus or an entity can take root. Upon further discussion, it seems that Erik had secretly been riddled with guilt over the break-up of his relationship. He put on a brave face, but in reality, the idea that he would not be a daily part of his daughter's life was eating him up inside. Perpetual sadness or guilt is like a flashing, neon vacancy sign for a low vibration, caustic energy being. Erik had unwittingly left himself vulnerable for this lecherous, dark entity to cling on.

There was also another elephant in the room that warrants serious discussion when speaking of entities. It seemed that Erik was fond of using marijuana as a means to relax and unwind. He wasn't a heavy smoker, maybe a few joints a week. It has taken many years to overcome my judgements around the subject, but now I have absolutely no attachment to the moral issue of drug use; that's an individual's personal choice. I do, however, see the world with a set of eyes that allows me to visualize the auric field, spirits and entity energies, so I can say beyond a shadow of a doubt, drug use leaves a user far more prone to attachment. This goes for all psychoactive drugs, legal or not, as well as alcoholic *spirits*. I can't even begin to tell you the number of regular users that I have had to clear from the dense vibration of entity attachments. I'm sure there is some eloquent and elaborate metaphysical explanation about the effects of drugs and alcohol on the vibrational capacity of the pineal gland, therefore causing a temporary portal of entry for the undesirables, but in my very best effort to keep it simple, let's just say *they leave the door wide open.* The frequency of intention has everything to do with the outcome as well. Someone using cannabis to heal cancer has a very different vibration to someone who is looking to escape the world for a while by getting high. It's *all* about frequency and intention and there is no action or reaction that is not based somewhere on the spectrum of the vibration of light, no matter how dim that light may be.

Understanding this has forever changed the way that Erik deals with the more difficult challenges in his life. It also caused him to re-evaluate his occasional recreational use of marijuana to 'escape and unwind'. From that day forward, Erik never experienced another black out.

Voodoo? Seriously?

The last thing I thought I would ever come across in the sanctity of my healing room in the middle of Ireland, surrounded by soothing colours and lights, chakra paintings and ancient Celtic wall hangings, was Voodoo. Don't get me wrong, at this stage you can probably guess that I never say never, but the day when the most fabulous Spanish beauty walked through my door and told me that she was sure that Voodoo was at play in her life, you could've knocked me over with a feather! I must admit, I was in new territory, but at the end of the day, darkness is darkness, no matter what the source.

Married to an islander from the Caribbean, this visitor told me of her most recent trip to the tropical shores of her husband's homeland. She had been invited to a ceremony, a drumming circle to be exact, where she became acutely aware, (a little too late) that a member of the circle was up to no good. She described a euphoric sensation that had first come over her body, nearly sensual in nature as the drums beat on in the background. Later that night, clear visions of the man from the circle appeared to her, disrupting her sleep and lingering in her waking thoughts. The energy was intensely sexual and she swore that she could feel this man touching her in the enduring dreams that were now making a nightly appearance. Her husband was the one who had explained that this sounded like a Voodoo curse. He had been present the night the 'spell' was cast and was highly upset that someone would violate his wife in this way. He, too, had been a guest and was not familiar with any of the drumming circle's participants. Voodoo was not something this lady had ever encountered in Spain or in any of her travels abroad. Her energy levels waned as she became increasingly aware that she was under some sort of spell. She hadn't even known this man, but he remained with her, even after she had returned to Spain. She couldn't focus, her appetite had disappeared, and it seemed as if this 'curse' was attempting to tear her away from her husband's love. She hadn't known where to turn. Was there anyone adept at dealing with this kind of disease? A friend had pointed her in my direction and she took the next flight out of Spain in search of answers.

A dear friend of mine had recently gifted me with a necklace of orgone; crystals, metals and copper attuned to my own personal frequency through a shamanic journey, then sealed in resin. I happened to be wearing it on the day this woman came seeking my assistance. The necklace was beautiful, a hand-crafted work of love and for that reason alone, I had it around my neck. Unsure of its purported protection qualities, I wore it anyway because it had been made and given as a gift of love. It certainly couldn't hurt…

After my very exhausted new friend had fallen into a relaxed, semi-conscious state, I did the only thing I know how to do…I surrounded her in love and declared her body a vessel that only recognises the highest good. I spoke rapidly, without fear and simply 'uninvited' whatever had attached itself to this woman, commanding it to leave her immediately. Sounds easy enough, but trust me, not showing fear isn't as easy as it sounds, especially when dealing with the really dark stuff. With God as my witness, the more I demanded, the lights began to flicker and a shadow of murky energy lifted up and shot out through her solar plexus, bouncing off of me then out through the ceiling. The orgone protection piece around my neck flew off and landed across the room with a heavy thud. It appeared to have acted as some sort of surge protector, much like one that would protect household electronics from a lightning strike or sudden rush of electricity.

As many times as I think I've seen it all, my own understanding is put to the test and what I think I know to be true shifts, yet again. The Spaniard was startled but not surprised; as she knew something in her life had changed the night she danced with Voodoo. Palpably different, sweating but clear, she was now free of a curse that most of us have would have never even contemplated as a possibility. She thanked me for having a mind open enough to try to help her find her way back to health. I'm still not sure how we did it, but this I do know...there is nothing so dark that cannot be extinguished by the eternal healing light of the Creator. Understand this; and you will always find your way back to love.

Pennies from Heaven

One of the greatest joys in my life is the loving friendship of my soul friend, my sister from another mother and my kindred spirit, Tricia. Deeply connected to Spirit, the Blessed Mothers and the Angels, Tricia shares her esoteric knowledge through writing fiction. If the truth be told, they may as well be true stories, as she has an uncanny gift for bringing characters to life, shooting arrows of emotion straight into a reader's heart with subject matter that is profound, current and intensely insightful. As an author, she has been instrumental in my career as a writer, as my friend, she is simply invaluable.

We have a saying between us when we're sitting in our jammies, fire ablaze, tucking in to some magnificent, home-made dish that my children would affectionately refer to as 'real food' (I'm not noted for my culinary skills). With elbows on the table, totally relaxed, we laugh heartily as we remark that "We's just folks!" This sentiment refers to the fact that we can be completely at ease with one another; no make-up, no formalities, no fuss. If one were a fly on the wall at times, they might say *no manners*! We laugh until we actually cry, we share our trials and tribulations, we plot and plan adventures, we talk about upcoming story lines for books and we eat all of the 'guilty pleasures' we want, because in the company of true friendship, calories are a figment of the imagination. Between us, we have plenty of imagination to spare.

One of the things I admire most about Tricia is the reverence and respect she had for both her mother and father. I never knew her mother, as she had passed a few years before Tricia and I met. Her father only passed recently so I had the great pleasure of meeting and talking all things nautical with this incredibly fascinating man! From WW2 Veteran, Lighthouse Keeper, Merchant Mariner to senior Tug Captain in the Dublin Port, he was full of the most splendid yarns. He made it quite obvious that Tricia's passion for captivating an audience with words was not only a well- developed skill, but an inherited trait.

When her dear mother died less than a decade ago, Tricia deeply grieved her passing. She and her mother had been like I am today with my own Mom. They took adventures together, talked daily and really were the best of pals. Her physical presence was terribly missed and while Tricia knew that her mother was safe in the hands of the Divine, she wanted a clear sign that her precious mother was alive and well on the other side of life. Tricia would regularly get messages which she distinctly knew were from her mother; clear communications in the form of personal sentiments between them and re-occurring numeric sequences that would appear, especially during times of difficulty. From the time I first met Tricia, her mom became a regular and welcome part of our conversations. Tricia would always remind me to relish in every precious moment with my own mother. For me, that's a piece of cake.

Sweet Helen, or Momma Helen, as Tricia calls her, was delighted to finally meet Tricia in the flesh last year. They are constantly exchanging letters, emails and gifts. We often video chat when we are having one of our infamous sleepovers. In short, they have adopted one another. When Mom first set foot in Tricia's house, it was like a homecoming. Tricia was genuinely delighted to have Mom in her home and Mom was overwhelmed with gratitude for the experience. She's not just Tricia to Mom, she is also Patricia Scanlan, international, best-selling author and one of Mom's very favourite, so this was an extra special treat and a really big deal for her! As I mentioned in the opening, books and authors hold a very sacred place in my mother's heart. Tricia is humble and may just be *folks,* but she is also an author who has touched so many lives over the years with the power of her transformative words and goodhearted deeds.

Truly, I have never known someone with such genuine veneration for the Mother energy as our Tricia. She is forever making reference to the Blessed Mothers, to Mary, to Magdalene and the ancestry of women who have shaped the Divine Feminine on this planet. Mom wasn't long in the door when she was shown one of my favourite photographs of Tricia and her mom, taken many years ago. Mom remarked about how beautiful she was, as if she were right there in the room with us while Tricia and I smiled at how 'Sweet Helen' really is so sweet.

Anticipating a wonderful sleep following a beautiful meal and endless gabbing the night of her arrival, Mom began her nightly ritual of pin-curling her hair for a perfectly presented coiffure in the morning. While Mom prepared for bed, Tricia and I enjoyed a cup of tea, the Irish elixir and tonic of all woes. It was a very special time for Tricia, *the author*, as she was celebrating the twenty-fifth, or *silver* anniversary of the release of her first novel, City Girl. She had gone into her library to get a copy of her book, Winter Blessings, a lovely collection of thoughts and poems, to give to my mother. I was standing in the hallway when Mom finished her bedtime prep.

She looked so adorable in her dressing gown and little night cap, neatly securing her curls into place. While chatting about the anniversary of City Girl, the three of us were there, in a semi-circle, and Tricia had just given Mom a hug, saying how much she missed her own mother's hugs. All of a sudden, a silver coin, an old Irish Punt, to be exact, fell out of nowhere at our feet.

Extraordinary in its own right, what really made this incredible was the fact that the Irish Punt has been out of circulation since the introduction of the euro in the year 2002. It wasn't like there were Irish coins lying around the place thirteen years later. This silver punt had materialised from thin air and hit the ground, just as we were speaking about Tricia's silver anniversary. I'd love to tell you that we were speechless, but as I'm sure you have surmised by now, being without words is not an affliction that Tricia, my mother nor I suffer from. We erupted into laughter, pure joy and certain celebration that Tricia's beloved mother was acknowledging her daughter's literary achievements. Talk about a clear and definitive sign!

One of my greatest pleasures is when other people get to witness, first hand, the Divine at work in their lives. It's lovely to read about it or to hear someone else share, but to be there when someone sees it with their own two eyes is priceless.

So often I have received messages from people all around the world telling me that they have heard from a loved one in the form of coins appearing out of nowhere. I've often wondered, why coins? Is it easier for a spirit, an energetic being to manipulate the physical mass of a small coin? Is the coin, itself, significant in some way? Who knows...But I do know this; I've heard that many accounts of it, I know it to be true. There were also as many copper coins as silver in the Irish Pound or Euro currency, so it was specific that Tricia's mom manifested silver as we spoke about a silver anniversary. Our loved ones are never far away and trust me, if they want you to know that they are there, they will even go so far as to drop pennies (or punts) from Heaven, to say "I love you and I'm always near."

The afternoon that I finished writing this story, I picked my girls up from school. After talking to another Mom in the parking lot, I opened my car door to get in when something small and shiny caught my eye. There, perfectly placed in the centre of my seat, was a brand new penny gleaming up at me. It definitely hadn't been there before and I wasn't wearing anything with pockets from which it could have fallen. I gasped out loud. My daughter, Jemma, had no idea that I had just written about pennies from Heaven as a sign from loved ones. She turned to me and in a very matter of fact tone informed me that the penny was from Tricia's father. "How do you know that?" It was *too* coincidental to be a coincidence. With that, my extremely sensitive and highly tuned in teenager shot me the exact same look that I give her when she asks the same question. Touche'. I could do nothing but laugh. I took a photo of the penny and sent it to Tricia, knowing she would be delighted by the synchronicity at play. Ten minutes later, I found myself taking a second photo. I pulled into my driveway at home, opened the car door, and there waiting for me as I put my foot to the ground was another shiny new penny. I had opened the car door...no penny. I reached into the back seat to get my hand bag, turned back around and boom...there it was. Thin air folks...out of thin air. I have stated several times that the Multiverse loves to make a monkey out of me whenever possible. Hadn't I just written about other people's experiences, other people's stories, so convincing and so many, that I knew it to be true? Hadn't happened to me, but it sure did happen to a lot of other people. Guess *they* figured a well-timed, personal experience of this phenomenon was in order. Wonders never cease and there's always something new to be understood, especially if we keep our eyes and more importantly our hearts, wide open and ready to receive.

A Mother's Love

Maybe I'm a bit biased because I live in the picturesque midlands of Ireland, surrounded by sheep and cattle, lush, green fields and miles of quaint stone walls, but I really do have a soft spot for country folk. They are hard-working, good-natured and always have a humorous story to share about most anything. Playing a bit of traditional Irish music around an open fire with the locals in a country pub is a little slice of Heaven for me. I'm at ease anywhere there is a genuine appreciation for a good pint of lager and a few Irish tunes. Country folk in Ireland tend to follow their faith more diligently than the average church goer, so doing the Stations of the Cross, collecting money at the church gate, attending mass each week in addition to the funeral of *every friend of a friend*, is simply their way of life. Much of the older generation still strictly adhere to the practices of Catholicism, and straying from the guidelines of the Pope's church would be a great source of anxiety.

I find with most of my senior patients in Ireland, there is generally one common denominator when it comes to any issue they are attempting to resolve, be it spiritual, emotional or health related…Guilt. It's not like it's a big secret; most of them will readily point the finger and joke about the good 'ol Catholic guilt. We have a standing joke in my office when I am asked why on Earth I came to Ireland to work. "It's simple", I always say. "When your job revolves around alleviating the fears and anxieties so often caused by self-persecution and guilt, I'll never be out of work in this country!"

There is even a specific frequency in the Solfeggio tuning forks I work with, attuned for harmonizing guilt and fear. Let's just put it this way, I've worn out a few of those forks over the years, here on the Emerald Isle.

Surrounded by photographs of prestigious past pupils, including world-renowned author, C.S. Lewis, a former Belfast schoolhouse turned healing centre was the setting for the timely liberation of a very distraught, elderly lady. Aggie's daughters had convinced their eighty year old mother that she needed assistance with her chronic depression. Aggie had come in to the city from her home in the country with great reluctance. Her daughters had a quick word with me before her session, explaining that for as long as either of them could remember; their mother had been surrounded by sadness. Diagnosed years earlier with depression, Aggie took a sedative and anti-depressant each day, as prescribed by her doctor. Concerned that their mother never seemed to get any better with medication, Aggie's girls wanted to explore the possibility that her 'depression' may stem from something that no pill could ever fix.

When Aggie entered the healing room, I asked her if she knew why she had been brought to me. She sheepishly laughed, telling me that she had only come to appease her children. Next I asked if she had been told anything about what I do. "All they said was I needed to have an open mind because you weren't any ordinary doctor. They said you had some kind of powers or something." The innocence of her country demeanour was both charming and heart-breaking. Once she had settled onto the table, I began to hear the voices. The story I downloaded concerned the source of Aggie's anguish and brought tears to my eyes. While holding her hand, I looked her in the eye, trying not to shock her too much with what I was about to say. It wasn't my words that would surprise her; she knew the story all too well, carrying its burden on her own for many years. I was conscious of the fact that this God-fearing Catholic woman would have to digest the fact that *somehow* I knew her darkest secret. I relayed her blackest memory, stored so deeply in her cells, nearly word for word.

Aggie had raised five children, the youngest of which had just turned forty. Her husband had been a hard-working man by day and a hard-drinking man most nights. He was aggressive and demeaning towards Aggie, his violent behaviour when he had drink taken, had often left her in fear for her children's safety, as well as her own. This hulk of a man berated Aggie for having so many children (all his children) and threatened her with murder on numerous occasions, if she ever *got herself pregnant* again. He was very matter of fact when he told her that he would kick her pregnant belly inside out, before wrapping his hands around her throat and choking her to death if ever there was mention of another child on the way.

Aggie found herself in quite the dilemma in 1960's, Northern Ireland. Her religion prevented her from using birth control and her husband regularly raped her after a night out on the beer. When Aggie fell pregnant after just such an episode, she found herself with the heart-wrenching decision of choosing between her sixth baby's life or her own. Unable to think of what life would be like if her other five children were left without a mother, under their despicable father's care, Aggie told a fib to her husband about her need to make an emergency visit to her deathly ill sister in England for two days.

It wasn't just the baby that was aborted on that journey; any remnant of good humour or happiness Aggie possessed, remained in the women's clinic in the U.K., never to be seen again. She returned home a broken woman, pouring herself into the care of her children, but never with a smile; her heart always heavy with the guilt of her life *and* death decision. Her husband never found out; if he had, Aggie surely would have never survived his wrath. She told no one; no friends, not even her sisters, and of course, her children would never know the truth about the source of her depression.

Aggie stared up at me in utter disbelief as tears flowed from her aging eyes. "How could you possibly know?" The unbearable grief was suddenly replaced with an unfamiliar sensation of relief;

the liberation of finally speaking of her pain out loud, even if it was with a total stranger. I took her hand and told her a different story. This time, the girl was only seventeen. She was just about to embark on the most exciting times of her life, having gone off to visit a college that her parent's had hoped she would attend in the autumn of 1987. Never having taken a drink to speak of, she had succumbed to the merriment of a campus party and had become heavily intoxicated. When guided into an empty room by a boy who had been flirting with her all night, she soon realised that they were not alone. In an instant, two sets of hands were tearing off her clothes, her cries for help unable to be heard over the loud music and laughter in the corridors of the dorm. Not only did she lose control of her safety and well-being that night, but she lost her virginity, as well. Three months later, when other freshmen were deciding on classes and potential majors, this girl was deciding whether or not she could face the responsibility of carrying the baby inside of her. She went on her own to terminate a pregnancy that would have taken her down a path that she knew she was not meant to take. The choice was difficult but it was the right one for her. No one ever knew.

For three years, she masked the pain of her decision with smiles and laughter. She found solace in words that her father had once spoken to her, concerning a different situation that had been far less serious.

"If you let continuous regret, remorse, self-persecution keep you from functioning now, if you persist indefinitely in feeling guilty and upset over something that is over, then you are behaving in a non-productive manner. Feeling guilty is not going to make your life any better. You can learn from this experience, vow to avoid repeating it, and get on with living now."

If only he knew just how valuable these words had been. Three years later, a temporarily fatal car crash would find this girl in another world. Surrounded by an indescribable atmosphere of peace and knowing, she reviewed her life in the loving company of her Guardian Beings. She had the opportunity to deeply explore the meanings of each and every decision she had ever made. Where there were gaps in her capacity to understand, her Guardians were there to enlighten her. Upon reaching the review of her eighteenth year on the planet, an in-depth explanation was given to her about what happens when a pregnancy is terminated, either by choice or by circumstances such as miscarriage or even still-birth. She was shown that in the perfect plan of life, if a baby is not going to be born, the soul who would have occupied the body of the child can choose to temporarily incarnate if it feels it can grow and learn from the experience in the womb. In turn, the soul *may not* occupy the body because the circumstances and resulting emotions are specifically and solely for the individuals responsible for the child's creation. Either way, the soul is always in charge. She knew in that moment that this information would later be used to alleviate the suffering of countless others who had faced the very same situation.

Aggie sat up on the table, her weathered hands trembling in mine. Well over forty years had passed since she had sentenced herself to a lifetime of guilt and shame. "That girl was you, wasn't it?" She had the sweetest look of compassion as she gently squeezed my hands.

"Indeed, it was, Aggie. It's time to let yourself off the hook. You may be eighty, but while you still have breath in your body, you are never too old to learn something new. You didn't do anything wrong. This experience brought you to this very moment of understanding your soul's own plan. What's it going to be?"

Her smile radiated in that moment and was one of the most beautiful things I have ever seen. I reminded Aggie that in the grand scheme of life, there are no wasted moments. I did not want to see her swap her decade's old regret of terminating her pregnancy to save her own life, for a new regret of having squandered the years away to her suffering and pain. Her heartache had been real, and an important part of a story that would lead her to a new understanding in the winter of her life. Time is irrelevant to a soul on a mission. When seeking to understand the inner workings of the human psyche and emotions, a soul thinks nothing about quantity when attempting to gain quality experiences. For me, it's moments like these that make me go home and drop to my knees in gratitude for *every single thing* that has ever happened in my life. With hardship comes growth, with pain, comes knowledge, with joy, comes celebration and no one of these is more important than the other when gathering the threads that will weave the rich tapestry of a life worth living.

Healing a Family Tree

If I have learned one thing over the years, if someone wants to communicate with me, time, distance or death is no obstacle. In May of 2007, Gene Touchstone began to get a metallic taste in his mouth. Despite feeling dizzy, this avid golfer went to play a few rounds before returning home dishevelled and disoriented. The following day, an emergency spinal tap revealed Acute Viral Encephalitis and Meningitis. This well-respected local pharmacist was now at the receiving end of massive doses of medication, affecting his organs, including acute renal failure.

The once vibrant husband, proud father of two, and grandfather of four, had been moved to the University of Virginia Hospital, where he was fighting for his life. When his doctor asked to speak with the family in the waiting room, not only did Gene's immediate family come forward, but his friends from college and his hometown all gathered around. His wife, Debbie, was overwhelmed by this act of love and support.

Gene's body would eventually recover, after spending weeks strapped in a wheelchair because he couldn't hold himself in a seated position. Debbie taught him how to take a shower again, to feed himself, along with every other small task that the able body take for granted. Spatial and directional amnesia due to right temporal lobe damage made even the smallest of efforts, exceedingly difficult.

During his physical recovery, the family tried all sorts of medications to improve his well-being. But this once calm and rational man was increasingly more agitated and irrational. His daughter, Wendy, expressed growing concern at the fact that Gene was no longer behaving like the daddy that she had once known.

His physical recovery had peaked, and in 2009, the Touchstone family watched a slow and painful decline that would eventually leave him in an indefinite state of disrepair and emotional unpredictability.

In mid-February of 2010, one of Wendy's children became ill, and she needed her mother's assistance so that she could continue to work. Debbie obliged, trying to convince Gene to make the three hour trip to Richmond with her. He refused to go, insisting that he would be fine while she was away for a few days. Debbie reluctantly went without him, organising for a family friend to check in on him while she was away.

On Saturday morning, Gene rang Wendy's house to speak to Debbie, but she was in the shower. She immediately phoned back but got no answer. She tried again; still no answer. She then placed a call to their friend who was keeping an eye on him, asking that he pop over to the house and check on Gene. At this point, Debbie had already packed up and started home, with a gnawing feeling that something wasn't right. As she drove, she was listening to Elvis Radio on satellite, when the song "How Great Thou Art" began to play. It was then that she knew in her heart, that her husband was dead. Gene was found on the floor of his bedroom at around 1 pm. The final decree was that he had died of myocardial infarction. Three days later, on my 41st birthday, Gene's body was laid to rest.

Gene's burial wasn't the only event to take place as I passed another yearly milestone. On the night of February 23rd, I had an unforeseen visitor at my birthday party. The spirit who had been embodied as Gene in this lifetime appeared to me in a *not so subtle* glowing light. He was anxious to share the circumstances surrounding his death, knowing that I would eventually pass this important information on to his grieving family.

Gene had been fully aware on a soul level of the circumstances surrounding his imminent departure. He expressed the fact that he had known that his wife, Debbie, simply could not have coped had he passed away, without warning, when he had first become ill in 2007. There were practical things she needed to be aware of, household affairs that needed to be in order, that otherwise would have put her under a strain from which she may not have recovered. Her learning was in his pro-longed death process, not in the chaos that would be created by a sudden demise. His children, Wendy and Steven, would have time to adapt, to desire to see their father at peace, rather than desperately hang on to a mind and body that bore no resemblance to the man they had known as Dad. Even down to the day of his death, he unravelled a well-orchestrated plan for the family that he had loved beyond words. His refusal to go with Debbie to Richmond meant that she would not have to be the one to find his body.

On a conscious level, Gene told me that he was not aware that he was about to die, but on a soul level, he had been completely cognizant of his impending exodus, not leaving out a single detail. By taking the time to turn up on my birthday, his burial day, he was making his final loving gesture to the family he adored. He had not been 'the real Gene' for quite some time. On the night of his funeral, the real Gene, the beautiful soul who had played his role so well, came back.

"Get on with it", he playfully asked for me to tell his wife, amongst other detailed and very personal revelations. He was eager for her to grasp 'the big picture'; the one that he now completely understood in his spiritual form. He wanted to support Debbie in a way so different to how he had as her flesh and blood husband. His appearance after death would start that ball rolling.

Five hours behind in Martinsville, Virginia, I phoned my mom and told her what had happened. Never surprised, but always intrigued, Mom acknowledged the enormity of it all. She is always so good about that. I asked her to give Debbie a ring the following day, pass on my condolences and tell her that I would be speaking to her soon. Mom had no intention of telling her why I would be calling, but a five minute conversation soon turned into an hour.

My dear mother is quite the healer herself. Her gentle nature, her non-judgemental tenderness, all created a safe space for

Debbie to open up and share her heart-ache. The timing was just right, and Mom ended up sharing a portion of our earlier phone conversation with Debbie. It would be the following June before I had the opportunity to sit on Debbie's back porch and tell her all.

Her daughter, Wendy, was there, and on that night, Gene made a second appearance. He encouraged his daughter to focus on making some personal changes in her thought process. Life had been tumultuous, and he made it very clear, using me as his conduit that he was completely aware of what had been going on in her world. These were things that I hadn't known until he literally whispered them in my ear, as Wendy sat right in front of me, validating each comment.

I asked both Wendy and Debbie, how much they really wanted to know about Gene's passing. They both agreed that they needed the entire story, no matter what that meant. What was revealed was the message of a soul plan leaving no stone unturned, one that created an understanding of life beyond death; one that these two women had never fathomed. He spoke of his beautiful connection with his grandchildren, and that he also knew that the day would come when his wife would allow herself the freedom to love again. No one would be like Gene, but why should Debbie experience the same type of love twice in one lifetime? The time would come when she would love as a mature, experienced woman, with her family reared, when her time was finally her own. The circumstances would be completely different to the day when a beautiful, inexperienced girl married her dashing, young sweetheart, embarking on the challenges of raising a family together. Debbie would have the chance to learn love in a different form, according to her deceased husband. While new love was the last thing on Debbie's mind, Gene was making it crystal clear that she would, in fact, love again. Can you think of any message more moving?

For me, Debbie was no longer Wendy's mom, as she had been when I was growing up. Gene's death had forged a friendship that I now cherish. Wendy and I had always been friends and shall always remain that way. Only now, we share something just a bit out of this world. Debbie also gave to me a morsel of wisdom that I have used with numerous people who are grieving the slow death of someone they hold dear. She has absolutely no idea how many lives have been touched with this one simple comment. In her infinite growth and understanding of her husband's death, Debbie made this profound statement.

"I had to live with my husband damaged, in order to let him go."

Following Gene's passing, Debbie spent a tremendous amount of time releasing, letting go and really trying to understand the circumstances around her relationship with her husband. Our own friendship was growing stronger and each time I would return to Virginia, Debbie and I would spend hours on her screened-in back porch, looking at her life and Gene's death from different perspectives. It was a time of great growth for Debbie, as her children were grown and her husband was no longer there. She had to face what I believe is a human being's most difficult challenge…to sit with one's self. Sounds easy enough, but day after day, night after night, to sit in the company of your own mind when the last forty something years of your life's focus has included the care of another soul…it 'aint that easy.

Debbie had an unusual scenario for an individual in her sixties. Both of her parents were still alive. In their nineties, Debbie's folks were still living, unassisted, in their family home in Danville, the next town over. For one who had nurtured children and a husband and eventually cared for him through his illness, it was probably a blessing in disguise that Debbie still had her parent's to look after. She was never afraid of their deaths, she knew that was inevitable, but there was the odd sensation of knowing that her core family would no longer exist. Her children would be there, of course, but the family unit that she had grown up in would cease to be, as her only brother had passed a few years earlier.

In February of 2013, Debbie's mom, Irene, was leaving a church meeting with a friend. She was in the passenger seat when the woman driving the car pulled out in front of a large truck, which struck Irene's side of the vehicle. She broke her arm and wrist and was very banged up, but managed to survive. After being released from the hospital, Irene was moved to a nursing home for rehabilitation.

In April, just two months later, Debbie's father, Howard, had a series of bad falls, resulting in bruising on the brain after a very serious injury to the head. He was admitted to the same nursing home as his wife but into a different room. Irene had not wanted to share a room with her husband of over seventy years because she said he talked too much! Howard's recovery was difficult, as he had to be restrained due to the brain injury. Both parents remarkably healed, therefore in June, Howard and Irene were able to return home under the watch of twenty-four hour carers. Debbie had convinced each parent that the other required full time nursing, so both would agree to the assistance.

In July, Irene told Debbie that she had experienced a most vivid dream in which God told her that she would die in two weeks. Debbie had gone to Danville to visit her folks with her sweet little Schnauzer, Lexi. Usually, Lexi would make a real fuss of Debbie's parents, snuggling up, looking for affectionate pats on the head.

Both Howard and Irene absolutely adored this little dog. On this day, the dog refused to go near Irene, as if she knew something was wrong. Later that same day, after Deb had returned to her own home, she received a phone call saying that her mother had suffered a stroke and was being taken to the hospital. By the time Debbie made the half hour drive back, her mother had sustained a second stroke and Debbie was faced with the decision of whether to have her intubated or to let her slip away on her own. A Do Not Resuscitate, or DNR, was in place and Debbie really struggled when faced with the decision. Her mother was suffering, but Debbie felt very strongly that her father should see the love of his life just one more time. The grandchildren were called and had the opportunity to see their grandmother again, but Debbie encouraged all to return home, feeling like she needed to sit with her mother's death process in her own way. She had the loving support and nursing expertise of her cousin, Nancy, and I had just arrived for the summer from Ireland.

"The most difficult and the most glorious thing I've ever done." This was Debbie's description of removing her mother's breathing tube. For anyone who has not experienced the death rattle, it can be terribly distressing as an observer. Human instinct nearly demands that you intervene, help the person to breath…do something, anything to ease the suffering. For me, Irene's death rattle was an entirely different event.

Before her breathing became terribly laboured, Irene had begun to demonstrate a feat that I have been fortunate to witness at a number of passings…including my own. There before me, as plain as day, Irene's spirit, her essence, her energy body, began to rise out of the body and hover. It was as if she knew that it wasn't necessary to physically experience her final hours in the hospital bed, hooked to machines and monitors. Irene's true self simply watched as her body began to wind down and prepare to expire. It was during these few hours that things became really curious.

For starters, the night nurse came in and introduced herself with an extremely familiar brogue. They say you can't go anywhere in the world without running into a Paddy, and indeed on this night, we had the luck of the Irish. Irene's nurse was brilliant; our instant chatter about her home in Ireland and things we shared in common put Debbie at ease and created a light-heartedness to the atmosphere in the room.

Irene's favourite church hymn was "Jesus Is Tenderly Calling". In the wee hours of the morning, my mother sat at her piano in Martinsville and played into the phone, as Debbie and I sang to Irene. The Irish nurse had looked up the words to the song and printed them out for us at the nurse's station. She watched with tears in her eyes as the room filled with the glow of the unmistakable presence of the Divine Light as we sang Irene through her passing.

Over the next few hours, Irene had flat-lined on nine different occasions. I watched her spirit disappear and reappear from its perch in the top corner of the room. I was fascinated by what took place during this time. When Debbie would try to hold her mother's hand when she was 'out of the body', she would get a terrible electric shock sensation. When she was 'in the body', Debbie was able to touch her without consequence. I tried it myself and twice got a jolt that nearly knocked me off my feet. It was as if Irene was highly charged when out of, yet still tied to her dying form.

I encouraged Debbie to close her eyes, wrap up in a blanket and snuggle into the armchair for a while. Mostly, because no matter how reverent the process is, the death rattles of a loved one can be terribly unnerving. She rested and I sat with Irene until the counts between breaths became so pro-longed that I told Debbie that the time had arrived. With a few final heaves of her fragile chest, Irene finally slipped into the beautiful beyond with her loving daughter by her side.

Debbie's mother had left written instructions as to how she wanted her funeral conducted. In the chaos of the final few days, Debbie was unable to find Irene's last wishes. She proceeded to carry out the funeral arrangements, the music and the readings, and much to her surprise, when she finally located the missing instructions, she had fulfilled her mother's wishes, down to the last hymn and prayer, exactly as she had stated.

Sitting on Debbie's back porch, we ruminated on her mother's parting from this world. It had been a beautifully heart-breaking occasion and now, she was wondering about how her father would handle being on his own. It was then that I shared with her that it would be a matter of weeks before her father would pass.

One week later, Howard was hospitalised with kidney issues. I went over to the now familiar halls of the Memorial

Hospital and set out to assist in making his transition as peaceful as possible, however long it may take. I used the Solfeggio tuning forks to clear Howard's chakras. When I flooded his energy field with 528 hertz, he smiled, put one hand on his heart and reached up with the other. Debbie's prayers were answered when Howard was able to return to his own home, to be the centre of attention or 'top dog', as she put it. His life had revolved around Irene, always putting her first and Debbie was so delighted that he would now be the focal point of everyone's affection. Debbie's son, Steven, came home and spent time working on physical therapy with Howard and he rallied for a few weeks. Debbie had moved over to her parent's home in Danville so she wouldn't have to continuously drive back and forth each day. Howard was in good spirits, particularly because on most occasions, his mental state caused him to think that Debbie was his wife, Irene.

One afternoon, Debbie had stopped by the home of her fiancé, Ben...Oh yes! The prophecy Gene's spirit had shared from the other side just a couple of years earlier; Debbie would love again... had come to fruition. Debbie had rekindled a romance with a sand box playmate from her childhood. Irene and Ben's mother had regularly taken strolls together with the baby buggies when Deb and Ben were tiny tots. The circle of life never ceases to amaze.

Debbie's dog, Lexi, had been in Ben's back yard when she was bitten by a copperhead snake, becoming extremely ill. Debbie was exhausted and hadn't even had time to deal with the grief of losing her mother before going into full-time care of her Dad. Debbie had to return to her own home for two weeks to look after her gravely ill dog. This gave her a much needed reprieve and a bit of time to catch her breath. Once little Lexi was out of the woods, we joked that she had 'taken one for the team'. From my perspective, I could see the space opening up for Debbie to begin to physically separate from Howard.

So often, when someone we deeply love is going through the death process, we want to be there, by their side to show our love and support. We often forget that in some cases, an individual might have a much more difficult time letting go of the body when surrounded by loved ones. This is evident in the stories we hear about family members sitting faithfully by a deathbed, holding vigil, and then going for a cup of coffee or home to take a quick shower and then getting the phone call that their loved one has passed. I experienced this with my own father, having sat by his bedside for weeks until a prophetic dream declared that he could not let go with me anywhere near. I literally had to jump on a plane and leave the country so Dad could pass. I then flew back from Ireland to the U.S. just two days later to bury him. Just because I know doesn't make me immune...

Debbie and Ben were due to go to a wedding in New Orleans, and she was distraught at the idea of leaving her father, but after many late night discussions regarding life and death, she understood that it might just be her presence that was preventing him from moving on. She had only been a few miles away and able to be by his side within minutes when her dog had been so ill. The trip to New Orleans would mean airplanes and a day's travel in order to get back to Howard.

The day before Debbie left for New Orleans, my mother and I went over to Danville to visit with Debbie and Howard. We were greeted by one of Howard's care givers at the door. The family was so blessed to have found the most loving sitters to be with Howard in his final days. The role of carer is one that is so important and can literally make or break the final, precious moments for a family. Loving and so kind, Debbie had a real treasure in her parent's care givers.

The afternoon is one I will never forget. My mother's last days with my father had been very much like what I previously described. My parents had been so close, my father so involved with my mother's life that he had to push her away in his last few weeks of Alzheimers. One of his carers had been there to witness his passing, not my mother. Paul, the carer, told Mom that he had never known my father as a younger man but he had seen what Dad used to look like, just before he passed. Paul described a morphing of sorts, in the wee hours of the morning, as my Dad's face became youthful just before the body begin to glow and his spirit lifted out. Not having ever experienced a death where he 'saw the light', Paul said that my father's death had changed his life forever.

Now, I was standing in Howard's room, only a year after my own father had passed. I called Debbie, the carer and my mother into the room. I knew in my heart of hearts that they would be able to see what was happening in front of me. The room lit up, there were tiny lights popping all around, like a miniature fireworks display. I watched the carer put her hand over her mouth. Debbie and my mother were softly crying and I sat in wonder at the misunderstandings so many have about the miracle of death. My mother, having missed her husband's grand exit, was now privileged to see the beautiful demonstration of a soul's passing from one realm to the next. The carer would no doubt ever see death the same again, and Debbie could let her Daddy go, knowing that this Divine process was perfect in every way. It was now only a matter of time…and Debbie's departure.

In a moment of flawless lucidity, Howard looked at me and asked, "When is she leaving?" He was ready to go home, but he knew that he couldn't take his leave until Debbie was out of reach. The following day, October 30th, Debbie left for New Orleans. On the 1st of November, Howard's carer called me to come to the house. I sat in those final moments with Howard and his minister, Jeff. A light began to emanate from Howard's crown chakra. Two luminous beings, distinctly not family, hovered nearby. Jeff, not only the minister, but a dear family friend, prayed with Howard and I sat in deepest gratitude to be so fortunate to witness this most auspicious moment in another human being's story.

I love the healings; the reconnections and the wonderful occasions I have been so privy to observe and participate in over the years, but to be present and to sit with death, the closure of a soul's time here on Earth, for me, is the grandest honour of them all.

When Debbie returned from New Orleans, we talked about what she wanted to do for her father's funeral. She kindly asked me to speak and it was then that she felt that it would be important to share the real events surrounding her father's passing. Howard had been a grocer, a WW2 veteran and a pillar of his community. Just two weeks short of his ninety-fifth birthday, there were very few of his closest friends still living. For those who were, Debbie felt that she could best honour her father by telling them what really happened...and so I did. The funeral was lovely and customary for the most part, until I stood in front of the crowd and told what had transpired on the afternoon when Debbie, my mother, the carer and I had watched the heavens open up, preparing Howard for his journey home. When I was walking out to my car afterwards, two gentlemen, lifelong friends of Howards, approached me and one of them spoke. "Young lady, I want to thank you. I want to thank you for telling the truth. When you get to be our age, you find yourself going to a lot of funerals. The preachers give some nice sentiments and thoughts about what waits for us in biblical talk, but this is the first time I've ever been to a service where someone told me what actually happens when you die. At our age, it's literally just around the corner. I can't tell you the comfort and reassurance you gave me today. Thank you for your honesty." His friend, dressed in a blazer with a WW2 veterans pin on the lapel, nodded and agreed. Debbie's instincts to share her father's story had been spot on.

The wrap up of this amazing series of events took place on Debbie's back porch. I'll never forget the wind chimes. When we would speak her husband's name an unmistakable tune would bang out, even if there was no wind; and the butterflies...the amount of butterflies not typical for late autumn in the foothills of the Blue Ridge Mountains. "Little Orphan Debbie" as she jokingly referred to herself, had come a very long way in her own understanding of healing since her husband's death in 2009. When he had first become ill, Debbie recalled crawling into the bed next to Gene, begging him not to leave her. Four years later with her own father, she had learned to respect the space enough to let him go peacefully. With Gene, she was hanging on for dear life; with her parents, she chose to proactively participate in their passings in a way that honoured them, as well as her own growth and understanding. When she realised that she couldn't be by her father's side in the end, she was able to step out of the way, gracefully allowing him the space he needed to leave this life behind. Her circumstances with her mother had required her presence and she had made herself available not only physically, but emotionally.

Debbie had done so much work on herself, opening up to a new understanding of what it means to heal the family tree. The time I spent with her was deeply meaningful in my life as a facilitator. The sheer privilege, the trust and the honour to watch her evolve has impacted how I work with others in a most beneficial way. Without her willingness and total honesty, this would not have been possible. Not long ago, Debbie summed up the loss of her husband and parents in a way that truly touched my heart.

"By learning to make peace with Gene's death and by allowing myself to find the joy amidst the sorrow of losing my parents, it's like closing a wonderful book and moving on to the next great story, rather than reading the last chapter of the same book, over and over, for fear of its ending."

If that's not understanding…I don't know what is.

AM I BLUE?

Lying in bed one autumn night a few years back, I decided that I would call upon *The Counsel*, for a bit of help with a little health crisis I was struggling with.

The who? Allow me to introduce you…

In December of 1991, I was involved in a 75 mph T-bone collision in which I had a near-death experience that irrefutably changed my life forever. After being greeted by two Beings of Light, guardians who had been with me since the dawn of my creation, I was able to experience an inconceivable review of the twenty-one years I had just left behind, resulting in my own decision to return to my life as Mary Helen. I was clearly informed that I would go back with an upgrade, enhanced if you will, able to connect with information that could potentially change the stakes in the life experiences of other human beings. I had communed with the 'dead' (and I use that term loosely) for all of my life. I was told that in addition to seeing, feeling and dreaming things before they happened, I would have the ability to gather the information stored in the cellular core and ethereal body of an individual. In essence, by temporarily reconvening with the higher vibration found outside of the earthly realm, I returned with an uncanny ability to access these higher vibrations at will, in order to extract energy and information to assist other human beings facing crisis of a physical, emotional or spiritual nature. With this knowledge came a Promise. I was assured that I would not be left to do this on my own. There would be assistance, guidance in a most tangible way, and all would reveal itself in good time.

The Counsel has been with me for so long, that I can't exactly remember when our clandestine meetings began. The communication started as voices; very distinct voices. Not like schizophrenic type voices wrecking my head at all hours of the day and night, but clear, precise and discerning words of wisdom and information that I otherwise would not be privy to, without their assistance. These voices were different than those I had always heard; the ones belonging to the spirits of people who once walked the Earth in human form, now physically deceased. Those communications are more like impressions, giving factual information of things that have been, things pertaining to their experiences and interactions while on Earth, in addition to insights as to what they are encountering beyond the veil. The other voices, those belonging to *The Counsel*, give me information relative to other people's stories, to me, to my teachings and healing sessions, to world events, past, present and future. Sometime during my mid to late twenties, I consciously made the request that the voices show themselves. That first interaction is branded on my mind for all eternity.

In the most sensational excursion of astral travel or being out of body, I found myself, my true self, in a space that gave the appearance of a large room. The truly curious thing was that the room seemed to breath, giving the feeling of enclosure, but there were no walls. There before me were nine of the most unusual and magnificent Beings I could have ever imagined. In all of the visits to follow, there would be twelve.

They certainly don't look like us. I liken my first meeting with The Counsel to a blond-haired, blue-eyed European seeing the tanned, reddish hue and dark, silky hair of a Native American for the first time. Or picture an African, who has only ever known her own kind, with ebony skin and ivory white teeth, first encountering the pale, yellowish skin and almond shaped eyes of someone of Asian descent. There was recognition of similarity, yet we were different. Each Being was contrasting in colour, skin tone, features and manner of attire. Whether this was for my benefit or not, I'm still not sure. Somehow clothing seemed unnecessary, yet most of them wore some sort of covering.

The one who struck me the most was feminine in nature, her skin the most alluring shade of pale blue, a periwinkle of sorts, with unusual markings that looked like intricate tattoo art. It was with this lovely life form that I felt an immediate kinship; as if I knew her, knew her homeland and knew that we shared something that I didn't necessarily feel when looking at the other members of this assembly.

Each of the nine was obviously from a different locale, and all were easy to distinguish as male and female. It wasn't until I later met the final three, that I grasped the true meaning of androgynous. These beautiful entities simply 'were'. There was a vibration and a sense of wisdom about them that made it impossible for me to label them as either male or female. They did somehow appear to be of the same origin as the exquisite Being of blue I had such a resonance with when I had met the first nine members.

In my mind, I was aware that each representative had their own indigenous forms of communication. Some spoke telepathically, others communicated with an audible form of frequency pitch and the others through some type of mouth-like orifice. Again, I think this was somehow for my benefit and not particularly out of necessity. They were loving in nature, yet serious in their thoughts and words, much like parents giving firm guidance to a child. They clarified that they had been providing me with information outside of the five senses since my birth. They also expressed that they had watched me grow, having to accept on more than one occasion that I might not find my way back to my chosen path this lifetime. If I hadn't, there would have been others to fill the space until I remembered, in this life or perhaps the next. I was by no means the only one they watched. Apparently, I was part of some sort of team.

"Did you cause my accident?" My first question was greeted with warmth and understanding.

"No, you did. You reached deep into your core and rediscovered your purpose. We only obliged your request for immediate change."

Whoah! It took a moment for me to get my head around the idea that I had requested such a bold intervention. The plan had been that if I had not managed to decipher my path and utilise the gifts with which I had incarnated (using my own free will), this accident would provide an opportunity for me to remember, once I had reached adulthood. I was speechless, but in my heart, I knew it was so.

The first meeting seemed, in itself, to last a lifetime. In truth, it was only one night by my clock. From that day forward, the voices now had faces.

I was certainly accustomed to being at their beck and call, filled with impromptu knowledge that always seemed to be able to sort out other people's problems. Why couldn't they help me with mine? I had never wanted to abuse or take advantage of this line of communication, and yes, I was dedicated to a life of service, but I was really finding it difficult to focus and stay clear for others, because physically, I felt so awful, myself. Pain, I was accustomed to; in my back, my head, etc. I had grown strangely familiar with the bodily fall-out from the accident as the years had passed; the broken neck, migraines, hearing loss, dysfunctional swallow, the lingering effects of encephalitis, the distorted rib cage and contorted pelvis, not to mention a list of allergies/sensitivities a mile long that had literally developed overnight. But recently, I had constant cramping, all-day nausea, not to mention a diet that had dwindled down to mashed avocado and rice. It was becoming more than I could handle. I needed help and I needed it fast. Ask and ye shall receive, right?

I couldn't tell you what time it was. The children had long been asleep. I was drifting somewhere between REM and my old pal, insomnia, when I sensed that I wasn't alone. I can't say I was afraid, but I was most definitely startled. Standing next to my bed were two Beings. Solid in form, they were certainly not like spirits. They were the same pale blue as the kindred, blue female member of The Counsel I described previously, only these two had no markings. In fact, there was no anything. Not a hair on their heads or anywhere else on their bodies. They were smooth and perfect.

The Beings were what I would call humanoid. They looked like us, only they didn't. At least six and a half to seven feet in height, their cranial and facial features were like ours, yet slightly larger, and in proportion with the rest of their bodies. Picture the motivational speaker, Tony Robbins; hairless and periwinkle. They communicated in silence, through thought, and it was then that I knew they had been sent in answer to my request. Nothing like this had ever happened before. In truth, I had never asked for assistance this way. They informed me that we were taking a little trip, but first, I would have to be prepared for travel because of the density of my human body. The Beings were calling me fat? I didn't like the sound of that, but I also didn't have too much time to think about it. The next thing I felt, was a distinct prick on the inside of my knee, as well as between my thumb and first finger. I had experienced markings like this as a child and in my teens. Now, as an adult, many markings would follow. The world suddenly accelerated and I was out of my body.

No time seemed to pass and there was no real sense of travel, just a whoosh at departure and an immediate arrival. There, before me, was the most spectacular waterfall I have ever seen, in person or in photographs. The spray of the water was cool against the balmy air, casting a magnificent rainbow the full length of the falls. Where in the world was I? It looked like a tropical paradise. So lush and vibrant, the place felt alive, like it was breathing in the same fresh air as me. Unspoiled by human hands, I wasn't too sure if I was somewhere that humans had ever been before, yet, I appeared to still be in my own body.

"Yes, this is your planet." They were reading my thoughts. "You know this place as Micronesia."

My two companions then drew my attention to a particular flower growing all around the falls.

"What does this look like to you?" They were kind as they questioned me.

"The flower looks like it has whiskers!" I replied, like a child lost in some kind of fantasy land.

"Remember this."

Whoosh....we were gone.

The next stop wasn't so pleasant. Definitely on planet Earth, I knew that we were now in a shanty town somewhere in an impoverished country in Africa. This time there were people. The surroundings felt unsafe even though I somehow knew I was in good hands. Sitting on the dirt, leaning against a temporary structure was a dark-skinned man that in my mind, I can still see as plain as day. He wore filthy cut-off jeans and what used to be a long-sleeved, yellow chequered shirt, with the sleeves torn off just above the elbows. He was out of it. Completely strung out on something; the colour of dark urine where the whites of his eyes should have been.

Before I could ask what was going on, one of my two companions placed what looked like a piece of litmus paper on the ground, about the size of a large floor tile. He produced a tiny vial of liquid and placed a drop on the 'paper', instantly soaking the entire sheet. The second Being snatched the unsuspecting fellow off the ground, standing him upright, and then planted his foul looking, bare feet directly on the paper. In a split second, the parchment went black, while the man let out a moan, not of pain, but of panic. Absolutely no-one seemed to see us. He would have appeared like a puppet on strings to those around him. Holding the man by the shoulders, the blue Being sharply turned him towards me. The whites of his eyes now sparkled and his pupils were no longer dilated. His body was soaked in sweat.

Whoosh...

I don't remember waking up. In fact, I don't recall having ever slept so well. The following morning, as I rubbed the sleep out of my eyes, I began to recount the most outlandish dream I have ever had in my life. The girls were now awake, and it was time to get ready for work and school. I went to the toilet, brushed my teeth, and then took off my t-shirt on my way in to the shower. It was my hand that I noticed first.

Between my thumb and first finger were two identical marks. It looked as if I had two needle punctures, or bee stings, already healed over. I was nearly afraid to look down. There, on the inside of my knee, next to a rather large bruise in the shape of a thumbprint, were two more marks, the very same as the ones on my hand. I stepped back out of the shower and sat on the edge of the bath. Not sure if I would faint, get sick, scream or cry out; I began to laugh. I tend to do that when I get nervous. A bit shaken, I went straight back into my room and grabbed my phone, taking a photo of my hand and the side of the knee, because surely to God, the minute I tried to show the marks to someone, they would have mysteriously vanished.

After dropping the girls to school, I went in to work and was greeted by my office manager, Maureen, cheerful as ever.

"The little pale face of ya'! What happened?" After years by my side, she knew 'the look'.

I hardly knew what to say, but the very best part of my relationship with Maureen, is that I can start any sentence with something off the cuff like...

"Ok, so you know *The Counsel*.... And there was no need to explain. She had been witness to or heard about pretty much everything that had ever happened to me in the last decade. Maureen listened intently, not getting overly excited, because with all she had seen, it would take something out if this world to spook her. I finished the story and then I showed her the marks. That was the first time I ever saw her visibly shaken.

In between patients, we tried to come up with every possible scenario. The most plausible was that my subconscious mind was trying to help me solve my own problems. Congruent with the possible dream I had created, maybe I somehow managed to mark myself by manifesting the pin pricks as hives or pimples or... It was far-fetched, and we knew it, but it was the best we could come up with.

During lunch, I began to Google waterfalls in Micronesia. Where was that? They said I would know it as Micronesia. These two obviously had not followed me throughout my entire life or they would have known that I am terrible at geography. This place was unique, so distinct; I knew that if I saw it I would recognise it. The rainbow mist was unforgettable, so it didn't take long before I was staring at it, right in front of me, on the screen.

Medal-A-lyechad in the state of Ngardmau; the highest and largest waterfall on the island of Palau; located in the Pacific approximately 800 km east of the Philippines, and 800 km north of Papua New Guinea.

Hmm…This wasn't the first time I had been directed to this part of the world by *The Counsel*, I quickly realised.

About a year earlier, there was a vision I'm still not so sure that I wouldn't like to forget. In the midst of 'conversation' with the elder Beings, I was shown images of a world map following the next round of dramatic Earth changes. Anyone who knows me well knows I can't stand that kind of stuff. Call it scars, cellular memory, 'catastrophobia' or whatever you like. I don't like anything to do with cataclysmic world events. It's too raw when you harbour the detailed memory of flaming asteroids, volcanic explosions and a great wall of water, just over thirteen and a half thousand years ago.

I don't know if *The Counsel* was simply sharing information, attempting to quell my fears or giving me knowledge that would be relevant in years to come, but there was a map, and while some of it was recognizable, there were some pretty heavy duty changes to our planet coming up. Now, the interesting component and I suppose the part that left me a bit calmer about the whole thing, was that I was shown, via previews of my own children's future lifetimes, as to how gradual these changes would be. They were rapid in the grand scheme, but not Hollywood apocalypse style. The change, for the most part, gave rise to the opportunity for people to migrate away from continuous flooding and shifts in the land. Some of the changes would be devastating, but over-all; we would certainly survive it as a species.

Very clearly, *The Counsel* made reference to a place on an island I had certainly never come across in my studies. Again, not so far from Papua New Guinea, is an island known as New Britain. I was shown a dormant volcano in a mountain range that *The Counsel* referred to as Sulu. Sometime, with in my lifetime, it would no longer be a sleeping giant. This would trigger a series of events that would set Mother Earth in motion for yet another massive clear out.

Once again, I found myself revisiting this corner of the world, this time in hopes that I would stumble across the true meaning of my visit from the Blue men. I then recalled the plant with the whiskers.

"Remember this." One of the Blue men had impressed in my mind.

A quick Google search and I had the plant in question. Orthosiphon Aristatus, also known as 'cat whiskers', is a bluish/white flower, native to several regions in the southern hemisphere. I must have been gasping aloud, because Maureen was now standing over my shoulder, watching as I pulled up more information about the plant that had been a focal point of the previous night's sojourn.

"Maureen, you're not going to believe this!"

She chuckled, and frankly, so did I, because neither of us could actually count the number of times I had started a sentence with,

"Maureen, you're not going to believe this!"

Also known as Java Tea, Cat Whiskers Tea is used amongst herbalists for purifying the blood, as an intense diuretic, as well as to treat diseases of the gallbladder, kidneys and urinary bladder. A big, fat, rapid detox is what it was. Now, I understood. The small vial of fluid that the Blue man used to saturate the litmus paper in the shanty town in Africa was a concentrated, liquidized dose of this potent herb. It also appeared that the leaves of this plant contained an unusually high quantity of potassium salts.

I was out the door, down to my local health food shop, Au Natural, in two seconds flat. My friend Susan Coleman is one of the most knowledgeable people I have ever met in the field of herbal and natural remedies. She would either know about it already, or quickly find out how to get the tea if she wasn't familiar with it. A few flicks through her catalogue and she located a source.

"Get me as many boxes as you can!" I was excited. The Counsel was obviously putting me on a detox program. When I returned to the office, Maureen and I continued to try and make sense of it all.

The conclusion we came to was that we really weren't sure what actually happened. Did I see the Blue men? Yes. Did I feel the pricks in my hand and my knee just before some part of me journeyed to two different locations far removed from my bedroom? Yes. When I awakened, did we actually see the marks in the exact spots I had felt them? Yes. Did the foreign locations and the plant I was shown actually exist? Yes. And most fascinating, the medicinal use of the plant was in direct correlation to my current health issue. Maureen and I agreed. Far be it from us to say the Beings weren't real or it didn't really happen. We were both also open to the possibility that my own subconscious mind had created the scenario (marks on the body included) that would lead me to the information that would eventually help me to help myself. Conclusion? There was only one way to find out.

After less than two weeks of taking around six cups a day, the excruciating cramps, the bloating, the belching and horrendous gas all stopped. The awful grip in the chest that felt like one, continuous heart attack, also ceased. My gut and I will forever be grateful to *The Counsel*, the Blue men, or the release of some deeply ingrained collective conscious memory of the effects of this plant on a human body dealing with Gastro Esophogeal Reflux Disease and Diverticulitis. I have since shared this remedy with countless others, who have also achieved lasting results.

This little morsel of material nearly wound up in the recycle bin, but I made an executive decision (you can do that when writing stories from your own life). I decided that there was no way I could leave it out following an interesting conversation that took place in my office not long after.

My very dear friend, Karen, had called by the office for a chat. As we were catching one another up on the news of our lives, Karen asked how the book was coming along.

"You're going to love this one, Karen. I'm revealing some of my favourite covert operations!"

Thinking she would react with pure excitement, instead she questioned me.

"Which ones?"

I'm finally going to talk about *The Counsel.*

OK.....and?

And I'm telling about the Blue Men.

Karen thought for a moment, then asked very seriously,

"Do you really think that's a good idea?"

Curious to know the reason behind her comment, I pressed for an explanation.

Karen is someone I value for her honesty, truthfulness and genuine concern when sharing her opinion. A vivacious, bubbly blonde with legs up to her neck, she is a great talker, but she is equally, a very good listener. I love our chats, her passion, and her inquisitive, open mind. I respect her opinion, so when she queried my decision to include the 'visit' from the Blue Men, I genuinely took her concerns on board.

She had no problem with the story itself. In fact, she loved that stuff. Her issue was surrounding the fact that I had put so much effort into establishing myself as a reputable doctor and healer. People who might really benefit from my work or my writing might be turned off by something as 'out there' as Beings from another realm. A belief in them was one thing, but an up close and personal appearance? I completely understood where she was coming from. Her forthright approach, as well as her ability to express a diplomatic opinion was from the heart and always with my best interest in mind.

Without making light of her interest in my welfare, I pointed to the cross that Karen wore around her neck. This symbol represented a story that for some, who may have never heard it, and even for many who have, could seem as outrageous as any myth, legend or Blue Men. She had grown up with this account of a period in history as part of her culture; it had become a personal truth. So, to Karen and many like her, there was nothing difficult about it at all.

A virgin birth foretold by prophets, to a mortal woman impregnated by a God, heralded by angelic beings from a heavenly realm. The mystical pregnancy produced a gifted, mysterious child, who incidentally was tracked down by three very wise men via a unique planetary alignment. History quickly lost track of a major portion of this avatar's life, only to see him re-emerge as a grown man, a healer, a prophet; the son of the one, true God. This man taught the way, the truth, the light, converting Godless heathens into fishers of men in just a few short years (that we are told of).

There were miraculous feats of healing and the controlling of nature, itself a promise of life everlasting, secured by a belief that this God incarnate, sacrificed his life for the sins of all mankind. Not only was he resurrected from the dead, he appeared to the living, eventually ascending into the heavens above, to take his place next to the throne of God, the Father Almighty, for all eternity.

I explained to Karen that it was important to me that I not share a narrative that would make people comfortable, but that I tell what actually happens to me, because in my numerous sessions over the years, a good few have had experiences with extra-terrestrial encounters. From the first day I put pen to paper, I made a personal vow of authenticity; to keep it real. There are many subjects that I covered in my first book, "Promised By Heaven", that I have been told brought great comfort, as well as an alternate perspective about life as we think we know it, to my readers. There are also a number of topics I have written about, that I know, for fact, have made more than a few people squirm. To leave out the uneasy bits, to forget that one night I drank too much, resulting in my inability to defend myself from rape as a teen, that I had two children out of wedlock, that I had multiple businesses that went bust, that after my partner fled the country, leaving me alone to raise two small children, I got stung with a stack of his bills that would sink a small country, that I allowed my own self-pity to contribute to the creation of a tumour in my breast, twice, that I have a string of romances that never quite worked out; to leave any of that out, while in turn, telling about the incredible visions, the awesome premonitions, the near-death experiences, the fascinating psychic activity, the privilege of communication with those in spirit, or the countless, mind-blowing, healing sessions, would simply be sensationally selective and inauthentic.

Everything that I have ever written for you is my truth. When the subject matter has been 'out there', even hard for me to digest sometimes, I have tried to give the most accurate interpretation, in addition to any other plausible explanations, whenever possible.

My sole mission is to create the opportunity for a different view on life through my own adventures as a human, thus far. I aim to remind people to grab their lives by the 'you know what', and drain every last drop out of all experiences. The events of my life have completely and permanently altered my opinion of me and my fellow man. My story is one of faith. My current beliefs barely resemble those with which I was raised. They have expanded; they are all-inclusive and lack the judgement necessary to be a card-carrying member of any organised religion.

Let's face it, history tells a gruesome tale of the consequences for those who do not believe in the same God worshipped by whoever holds the power or the money. We are slowly evolving, and religious institutions based on fear and guilt are crumbling all around us. The one constant that prevails is the message of love. Love of self, our fellow brothers and sisters in this world and beyond, and the Source from which we all originate. I feel that as we discover more about what really happened in our past, catastrophically, geologically, and through the evolution (and possible enhancement) of our species, the state of tremendous fear that we live in will begin to shift. We are a world that is always waiting for the shoe to drop. We are already in the moment that so many are waiting for. As my cousin, Nicki, an extremely gifted healer from the foothills of the Blue Ridge Mountains would say in a southern accent as thick as blackstrap molasses… *"That shoe done dropped, people!"*

I thank my friend Karen, because her gumption to question made me realise just how important it is that we listen objectively to every story and view the human experience from as many different angles as possible. Question everything. Restore the elderly to the elders they once were, while supporting the work of the brilliant young minds that are currently incarnate and capable of innovative ideas that can further advance our fledgling species.

Faith is not a synonym for foolish, nor does faith require that we blindly walk through life, too afraid to raise our hands and ask the really essential questions. Faith can move mountains. So can bulldozers. A little bit of both is called evolution.

Alienated

As I have now told the story of the Java tea and my true blue friends, I am reminded of the privilege I had to be entrusted with a brilliant account of an out of this world visit, experienced by one of my patients. Vivian came to my office when I was still actively practicing Chiropractic a few years ago, checking in at the desk just like everybody else. When it was her turn to be seen, she closed the door behind her, speaking in a hushed tone. Intrigued, I listened carefully as she started her introduction with,

"You'll probably think I'm stone mad, but I've got a back pain that I doubt you've ever come across before."

Vivian proceeded to explain that she had been subject to a very unusual encounter several months earlier. In the very early hours of the morning, somewhere around 4 am, she had been waiting for her husband to return home from his job as a taxi driver. When he was finally tucked in beside her, fast asleep, Vivian was stunned by a blinding, bright light through the bedroom window. She was immediately aware that someone else was now in the room. Unable to speak or move any of her limbs, her husband continued to slumber. While very startled, Vivian recalls that she knew she would be OK. Whatever was happening to her did not feel malicious, albeit intrusive. When she became aware that the presence had moved on, Vivian found herself able to move again. Without delay, she woke her husband. Fortunately, for her sense of sanity, he saw the bright light, just as it shot off into the night sky.

Soon after, Vivian began to have severe pain in her lower back. In her hand, she held MRI scans that had been ordered by her doctor in attempts to get to the bottom of her complaint. This is when things got interesting. Vivian recounted the day that she was called in for the final report on the scans. Her doctor fumbled through their conversation.

"I've never seen anything like it, and I simply can't tell you what it is. There is a perfect, circular cavity of tissue missing from the spinal cord at the base of your spine. It's as if a slice was removed by some instrument. The only possible explanation is that it must have been there all of your life. You were probably born with it."

Vivian knew better.

"Yeah right, the flawless disc shaped hollow in my spinal cord just happened to start hurting right after the bright light and paralysis in my bedroom."

Vivian kept searching my eyes as she relayed her story, looking for judgement or a hint of disbelief. She got neither.

"Vivian, it's as real to you as my experiences are to me. I have no reason to doubt you. I'm here to help in any way I can. I will never forget the look of gratitude on her face. This had been a life-altering occurrence. It was the moment that redefined her entire belief system. With my hand on my heart, I could write an entire book dedicated to similar reports from people just like Vivian; everyday folks with families, jobs, homes, and seemingly 'normal' lives, who are keepers of their own clandestine encounters, too afraid to speak out, for fear of ridicule or worse.

So many people are terrified of being judged, with great reason, I might add. History has been very unkind to those who dwell outside of the mainstream; the heretics, the visionaries. I thank my lucky stars that part of the agreement I made when dedicating my life to this work, was that I would never be plagued with concern about what other people thought of me. I also acknowledge the fact that this hasn't always been the case. I grew into this mind-set following my near-death experience.

First, do no harm. Speak with integrity; create a sense of wonder and passion for those who seek guidance, always respecting every individual's right to his or her own beliefs. Most important, constantly remind people that it is more than OK to reconnect with their own divinity. After that, who cares if anyone thinks I'm nuts? This quirk in my personality has truly served me well.

In my opinion, the vast majority of our species has amnesia. We also have a tremendous capacity for selective hearing, seeing and the judgement of others who don't think or act in the same way that we do. Luckily, the courageous and inquisitive nature of many stewards of humanity, continue to propel us forward in the search for meaning, creating such instability in the status quo that people are finally beginning to wake up. There is evidence all around us that our current value systems, the very ways in which we conduct our lives and interact with our environment are all changing at lightning speed. Thank heavens for the tenacious research of many brave souls, willing to trade the positive accolades of fame and glory for a better understanding of our posterity and the mythology surrounding it, regardless of the consequences. I wish to throw my hat into that ring, forever more. For eons we have been taught that as humans, we are sub-standard in some way, unworthy or incapable of connecting with our origins and handling the truth about who we really are. We have become a product of the anaesthesia we have been fed by the powerful few. I, for one am ready for the wake-up call. Understanding is where we will find our healing.

Senior Moments

There are a few phrases I have simply had to erase from my vocabulary over the years. "You're not going to believe this, Mom" or "The strangest thing happened during the night" and my all-time favourite, "If I said this out loud I'd be locked up." So many miraculous occasions I've witnessed, extraordinary people I've come across, astonishing (*not*) humans I've encountered, the sudden influx of new information that shifts life-long paradigms in a moment; for these and so many more reasons, my mind is open to any and every possibility. I am now the adult version of the precocious little girl who used to frantically wave her hand in Sunday school, refusing to accept "because the Bible tells you so" as a valid reason for things that didn't quite add up.

I'd like to share with you **the most bizarre** dining engagement I've ever had to date, while not excluding the possibility that at any given moment, *the powers that be* can always up the ante, raise the stakes and land me in a situation so outlandish, that this story I'm about to share would seem like a picnic in the park. For now, amidst the physical and emotional healings, the past life sessions, the out of body excursions and every other paranormal episode I've ever stumbled upon, this is ranked up there with the strangest amongst them. Despite the fact that I've been dealing with this kind of carry on for fifty years now, I will never lose my child-like wonder when it comes to seeing a new angle to the supernatural. I really believe that's part of the reason *they* gave me the job…

The setting was Glasgow, Scotland. I had travelled over from Ireland with my trusty side-kick and agent, Mairéad. After attending a conference all day, listening to the presentations of some well-known speakers and authors, Mairéad ran into an old acquaintance as we were leaving the convention centre. The two ladies were delighted to see one another and after a quick catch-up, they organised for us all to meet later for dinner. Mairéad grinned like a Cheshire Cat as we walked back to our hotel to freshen up. "All I can assure you," Mairéad teased, "You will never have another meal like it." I was now, wildly intrigued.

We made our way back to the restaurant, which was open and spacious. The company was quite unusual, to say the least. A few tables over, publishing powerhouse and metaphysical author, Louise Hay, was enjoying some quiet time away from the crowds, while Doctors Wayne Dyer and Brian Weiss waved to her as they walked by. Anita Moorjani, a captivating new author and speaker, had just made her debut on the world stage of metaphysics earlier in the day. To say the atmosphere was sublime is an understatement. But believe it or not, sitting in the same restaurant with some of my favourite teachers/authors, actually has nothing to do with the story, it merely paints a picture of how surreal life can become in an instant.

Mairéad and I walked over to a table, where her friend was waiting. She was a most intriguing character, but as far as appearances were concerned, Rose was fairly non-descript, really. She looked like someone's granny, the really fun-loving, active type of nana who had managed to make it into the golden years relatively unscathed. She had already ordered, even though we were on time, because she was just like that. She was hungry; Rose wasn't the type to wait and made no bones about it, so her food was arriving just as we were. A massive steak dripped over the sides of the plate. Generous portions of mash and veg adorned her sizzling sirloin and she immediately tucked right in. She would occasionally pause to take a swig of red wine to wash it all down. Within seconds, there was a food stain on her wrinkled, cream coloured t-shirt, which hung loosely underneath a dull grey cardigan atop a pair of polyester black trousers. I imagined that she was the type of woman who was sturdy, well-travelled, well-educated, having long gone past the need to please in relation to her appearance. There were far more wrinkles in her clothing than on the face which had taken on the world for nearly eighty-five years. When she spoke her voice was strong; it had to be, as she was inclined to eat and talk simultaneously. I was absolutely captivated by this woman from the word go. She was eccentric, unconventional and oozing with charisma. Little did I know, underneath her innocuous and seemingly bland attire, was the most unexpected individual I could have ever imagined.

Not one to mince words, Rose got stuck straight in to a most unusual conversation. Mairead, ever the lady, sat bolt upright, her lovely eyes a little wider than usual, as Rose spoke to me and attempted to turn my life on its proverbial ear.

"I want you to close your eyes." Even if I hadn't wanted to, she was the type of person, I could tell, who usually got what she wanted. "Hold out your hand and tell me what you feel." My eyes had barely shut when I felt the heavy, disc-shaped object Rose had placed in my hands.

"What is it?" I was feeling its rough surface with my thumbs as I asked.

"You tell me, you're well able", she replied as she continued to chew, sounding more like the granny persona that matched her appearance.

It didn't take long before I knew in the core of my being that this object was not from Earth. It had a palpable, distinct vibration and there was something raised around its perimeter.

"This isn't from here." Although I had no idea what it was, of its unearthly origins, I was somehow certain.

"Very good", she remarked, like an old school marm."You are right, this isn't from here and in a minute, I want you to open your eyes and tell me if anything on this object looks familiar."

Curiosity was killing me and Rose laughed as I opened my eyes. I observed a burnished, bronze coloured disc, resembling a large hockey puck in shape and diameter.

"Look closer", Rose encouraged.

My mouth hung open. I looked up at Mairéad as she leaned across the table, her eyes nearly bulging out of her head at this point.

"What is it?" Mairéad was on the edge of her seat waiting for the big reveal.

I immediately looked over at Rose. "Who are you, lady?" I was flummoxed and a little uneasy as the tone of the entire conversation suddenly shifted.

That wasn't quite the response Mairéad had expected, and she flashed me a look. Anyone who has ever been a mother has this look built in to their factory settings...*the eye*. That not so subtle glare that says you've crossed a line and you better get yourself back over it right quick. Mairéad was worried, rightly so, that I might offend, but true to form, Rose began to chuckle and said, "I thought you would find this...interesting!"

Encircling the outer edge of this extra-terrestrial lump of material; not metal and not stone, were a series of symbols, raised high, as if embossed in to the disc. My shock had come when I realised that I recognised the symbols. These were the ancient encryptions that had first appeared to me in a series of visions many years earlier; the same ones the Atlantean woman had been in charge of protecting in my first past life flashback, when I was five. These were the symbols that Dr. Lew Graham, my friend and colleague had spent the entirety of his adult life searching for. He was well aware of the first three and when we met fifteen years ago, I had been able to give him the remaining nineteen, inclusive of a 'primer' that interlocked with each one individually. He eventually wrote a book entitled Gnosis, explaining the origins of these symbols on Earth, their pre-Atlantean roots, inclusive of an alternative version of the history of the world at that time. I first published these icons in book one of the "Promised By Heaven " trilogy, when it was independently published in Ireland and simply called Promised. To my knowledge, this was the first time these ancient cryptograms would have ever been made public.

Rose quickly jumped in, stating she knew all about my publication of the symbols. She said things like "*We've* been very interested in what you have shared and have a keen interest in filling in some of the gaps for you. She laughed and said, "We're actually working for the same team, you know, I just don't think you have fully come to realise this yet."

My first thought was that she knew *The Counsel* I work with. Well apparently, she knew *them* and a whole lot more. She explained that it was time for me to know the truth.

The truth? Is there such a thing? And why was it suddenly time for me to know it? I got the distinct impression that everything I thought I knew was about to blow up in my face…again. Actually it didn't, but I guess you could say, anything I had ever known before, dramatically expanded before the main course had even arrived.

Rose said that *they* knew that I had worked with international government officials who had confided a wealth of classified information about how this planet operates. This was true. I have confidential *confessions* from some reputable higher ups locked away in my memory banks that would completely deconstruct reality for a majority of Earth's population. I always considered it part of *the job*. I guess I've been exposed to so much in the multitude of sessions I've facilitated, I never really sat down and pieced it all together; feeling like my role was to hold space, continue to raise vibrations and bring as much light to the human condition as possible. In a moment of clarity, as Rose spoke, it was as if my wheels set in motion and I glimpsed the magnitude of the collective insider information and *knowing* that has been shared with me over the years.

"*We've* heard you speak of duality, of the dark and light here on Earth on numerous occasions. Do you actually know what that means? Have you truly grasped the significance of this?" I'm pretty sure I was starting to sweat beneath my fleecy jacket as her intonation reinforced the fact that like it or not, she was going to tell me what she wanted me to hear.

"You have been working with *The Counsel* for many years now. The fact that other beings assist, protect and act as catalysts to those here on Earth isn't new to you." She was right. For a long time I had been very secure in the fact that we aren't doing anything alone or without assistance. I had never given thought about the far reaching implications of this until I met Rose.

"You also teach that souls congregate in groups, kindred spirits looking to accomplish similar goals while incarnate on Earth. You explain how they choose their paths; how they agree to assist one another, playing specific roles in order to advance growth and spiritual development." So far, there was nothing I could argue with.

"There is a missing piece of the puzzle that *we* think is appropriate for you to learn about now. You are correct that Earth is a dichotomy of dark and light. No other place in this galaxy can provide the simultaneous experience of pure love and exquisite beauty coupled with violence, hatred and destruction. This truly is a unique set-up. What you need to understand now, is that there are *teams*, multiple beings, human and those not from this world, whose priority is to work together to provide this dichotomy to the souls who come to Earth." Rose sat back and looked straight through me as she continued. I didn't flinch.

"It is human nature to wish for world peace, to pray for unity, to hope for the world to live as One. That's not the purpose of this planet and what it has to offer. It is also the reason that religions come and go, 'Saviours' are created, Holy texts are enshrined and humans are always looking forward to a time when there might be Peace on Earth. What they fail to realise is that there has never been total Peace nor will there ever be, at least not until the construct of the planet is changed through a conscious collective and unified shift in the human vibration. Just as the species has never managed to annihilate itself, *because we won't allow it*, this schoolhouse for hearty souls promises the experience of duality. Duality or separation from the Source of All That Is, is the mythology that spirits come here to engage in. The opportunities for expansion and the rush of temporarily believing *that it's even possible* to detach from perfection, that's what it's all about. *We're* all about enhancing the human experience so that souls can maximize their time here."

Rose used an example that really hit home for me. "If you were spending your hard-earned money to book yourself on a cruise, there are certain things you would and would not want to experience whilst on your trip. The idea of all you can eat buffets may be appealing, as well as a location awash in sunshine, maybe some scuba-diving, spa treatments, dancing, a few shows and a cabin with an ocean view. If you paid for these extras, there is a cruise director whose job it is to ensure that you have these experiences. There is, in essence, another being focused on the intention that you get what you signed up for.

Maybe an individual wants to take time away from work and family, to travel to a third world country, to feel as if they can really make a difference, teaching, feeding and caring for the health and well-being of impoverished children, fighting injustice and bringing awareness to atrocities that are not a part of their own, personal reality. There, too, would we find beings whose purpose is to make sure that these expectations come to fruition. Humans are often guilty of confusing *what they think they want* with *what the soul has requested* in order to expand."

My mind was blown by the total randomness of the messenger and surroundings more so than by the information. Rose continued to explain the roles of these teams of beings whose mission is to create the illusion of bi-polar division; the light being no more important than the darkness. Servants of humanity who would as frequently antagonise or stir the pot, as create the miraculous moments, are all over the planet, guaranteeing that an incarnate soul can have the opportunity to live what they have come here for. I had known these things, experiencing many flashes of this reality over the years, compartmentalizing each experience for my own sanity, I suppose. Rose was now weaving this tapestry together, right in front of my eyes.

"Opportunities are what *we* create; however, 'free will' dictates whether a soul chooses to use these gifts or not. So few actually realise the power they possess to create, therefore we continue to assist until all of the species evolves enough to change the program." Program? That word I had casually used so many times before had just unnerved me in a most unexpected way.

Rose explained that her appearance was by design. She looked innocent enough so when she travelled on any of her multiple passports, no one ever questioned the old granny figure who was slipping into the Middle East, on to the African continent, or over the Russian border. When rallying a group of women for an uprising in Syria or sweeping the floors in an American college at the time of a random shooting spree, bringing the tools necessary for clean water to a village in Nigeria, or sparking a revolution against a dictatorship in Nicaragua, Rose had played "Angel and Devil" for the entirety of her adult life as a member of this team. I was, in that precise moment and time, feeling the exact experience she was describing; parallel feelings of wonder and outrage.

"We are eternal, and as you have said yourself, nothing can actually harm who we really are. The personal enlightenment, the growth, the love and understanding that can be achieved from living in the duality is beyond explanation. To be in it, not of it; to understand that the pain and the pleasure are equally important to the soul seeking the human experience; this is where we will find our personal peace. When we lose an individual, or as I have witnessed on so many occasions, an entire community of people, it is difficult to see a higher purpose or the greater good. We must always remember that each of these souls came into this world knowing that this would be their fate. The conscious mind over-rides this knowing in order to allow them to engage and permit a difficult scenario to play out, but the dynamic, loving and omnipotent souls who are at One with their own divinity, whole-heartedly agree to come in to this world to provide and obtain these experiences. To one who knows that the physical form is merely a vehicle with which to traverse the incarnations of Earth, this is an extremely simple concept. When a soul finally figures it all out, they have the option to return to the Earth cycle to assist others in their growth or to move on to a different field of vibration. Trying to change this set-up before our species has collectively elevated to a higher frequency makes about as much sense as an aspiring chef wanting to change the curriculum at Harvard Law so she can go there to learn how to cook."

With that, Rose excused herself from the table. Mairéad was silent. I stood up not quite knowing if I should thank or restrain Rose. She assured me that in time this would all make perfect sense. For now, my task would be to find a way to digest then deliver this information to those who were ready to hear it. Many who read this will skirt right over the details and move on to the next chapter. There are those who will experience the proverbial light bulb moment. For some, anger, fear or disbelief will set in. For others, a knowing nod will be the response.

Rose kept in touch via email; very strange emails, I might add, containing cryptic messages that would leave a trail of clues as to where in the world she might be. I will never forget the day, several years later, when an email arrived from a name and address I had never seen. It appeared to be from a friend of Rose.

"I regret to inform you that while in service to humanity, our dear friend Rose, was run over and killed by a black SUV during operations in the Middle East. You were on her list of contacts in case of emergency. I am sorry for your loss. She will be greatly missed."

When I attempted to respond to the email, it simply bounced back, as if the address was no longer valid. Although we had never met again in person, Rose always kept in regular contact and I would sorely miss our correspondence. As for the black SUV? How absolutely appropriate and predictable... Rose's death had become a cliché.

I have shared this story with a few friends, who found it extremely disconcerting that beings would 'interfere' with the free flow of life. Quite the contrary, according to Rose; there have been ever so many times that this 'interference' may have allowed the human race to continue to exist. Comments have been made comparing us to puppets on a string, or the butt of some sick cosmic experiment.

To be loved enough by the Divine, to be privileged enough to take on an earthly shell in order to walk through this world for the soul's personal gain, hardly qualifies us as cataleptic puppets doing the personal bidding of some unwavering Master. The memory that impacted me most at the time of my near-death experience was that the separation of 'God and Man' is as much a part of the duality illusion as every other dark and light, good versus evil scenario we have here on Earth. To truly embrace self-love amidst the chaos and carnage on the Earth plane, is to express the highest vibration of love, with the ultimate realisation that we've been creating our lives all along. In essence, we *are* the Divine.

The possibility that we haven't left ourselves on our own to navigate this world, makes perfect sense to me. People have no problem believing with all of their hearts that Angels or other Heavenly Beings can manipulate circumstances in their favour. If part of the experience we come here for is to traverse not only the light, but the darkest, most painful of ordeals, does it not stand to reason that someone or something might assist with this task, too? When sampling this manuscript around prior to publication, a few interesting events occurred. There were several folks who got to this section and responded quite strongly. One set of friends even maintained that I had been fooled by 'dark energies' since birth; that my Grandfather Judge and all 'other-worldly' beings that I have encountered since my accident were not who they said they were. These same friends went as far as to insist that I renounce my Grandfather or *prove* to them that I'm not working for the Dark Side. If I could not or *would not*, they would cease all communications. I made the choice easy for them.

Another highly respected friend wanted to broach the subject that the dear Rose was most likely a Reptillian, a member of the humanoid, shape-shifting extra-terrestrial race purported to be controlling a majority of political activities on this planet. He felt that what Rose had described to me, sounded more like a Reptillian agenda than the way Earth is actually meant to function; an interesting observation and an opinion that I respect and believe he is perfectly entitled to have.

For me, telling Rose's story, along with all of those before it and those yet to come isn't about making emphatic declarations. I have attempted to share every encounter with the miraculous moments from the wide-eyed observer's point of view. To tell you that anything I have witnessed is absolute would be about as productive as trying to change your political allegiances with a single post on social media. Different experiences, observations and sentiments assist in helping other humans to see outside of themselves and their own 'fundamental truths'. The whole point of the exercise for me is to remind folks *never say never*. I, by no means, have seen it all, but if what I have seen has taught me anything…what we *think* we know as truth doesn't begin to scratch the surface of what is actually happening in the world(s) around us. To understand this, I have come to believe…is the truth that can set us free.

Understanding is also the New Forgiveness

I feel that a phenomenon I have regularly observed over the years is worth mentioning at this point. Initially, this book was to be called Understanding is the New Forgiveness. As the stories began to flow, I realised that while the title was catchy, it was limited. Forgiveness is a tricky word, really. It has been tossed around by religious and new age thinkers, alike. Deeply flawed in its implications, in my opinion, I opted to change forgiveness to healing, to best represent what I have observed as a facilitator. A trend began to develop some years ago, as I noticed an increase in the frequent appearance of a particular complaint. People who were totally switched on, open-minded and ready to transform their lives were talking to me about the tremendous amount of work they had done on 'forgiveness', yet they were still sick, distraught and failing to move forward. I began to observe a pattern amongst people who had been traumatized by rape, abuse and betrayal, to name a few, having dedicated so much of their precious time and energy to forgiveness of those who they felt had damaged them in some way. They were encouraged by religion, motivational speakers and self-help books to 'forgive in order to heal'. What I noticed was that the most diligent individuals, the ones who had dedicated their All to forgiveness, were the ones who seemed to remain engulfed by physical illness or emotional strife. If forgiveness is the key, I wondered, why are they still sick?

I found that a vast majority of those who exhibited this tendency also shared another thing in common. They felt as if they had failed themselves in some way because of their inability to fully forgive. Imagine a grown man who was so severely molested as a child that a single day does not pass without a portion of his energy and thoughts reverting to his abuser. Unable to grasp how an adult or teen could do something so horrific to a child, he is then led to believe that unless he forgives, he will not be able to move on with his life. As far as I'm concerned, this confusion between forgiveness and letting go of a damaging thought process about the past is what actually sets people up for failure, every single time. I am constantly explaining how Divine and loving souls agree, prior to incarnation, to play different roles in our lives; some loving, some unkind and some that are so challenging it's difficult to conceptualize with our human minds that we could have played any part in agreeing to, much less creating such hardship for ourselves. I always remind people that in between incarnations, we leave the confines of the five senses and are creating scenarios for our growth and soul evolution from a place of empowerment, omnipotence and Divine self-love.

Forgiveness requires the belief that another individual can actually harm who we really are; that we believe any action that is painful or challenging, is not equally as meaningful to our development as the beautiful and sanctified moments. To convince someone that they will not heal unless they forgive is quite possibly one of the greatest deceptions known to modern healing. Religions have run away with the concept, creating a middle man, or code of ethics that requires constant apologies for simply being a soul residing in human form. The idea that one cannot access the Divine unless X, Y or Z are first evoked is, in my opinion, flawed. It is the fastest train to disempowerment I've ever seen, but as I have witnessed, that train is full to capacity within many religious and spiritual disciplines. A simple change in perspective can take an individual who is struggling with physical or emotional well-being, and place them on a path that no longer requires self-flagellation disguised as an inability to forgive. To forgive is human; to understand that it's not the same as letting go, is Divine.

Grace and Opportunity

In my household, I have raised my children to understand that the proverbial 'box' that is so often spoken of in everyday metaphors, such as those who are 'in the box', or those who think 'outside the box', or those who want to collapse 'the box', can be an integral part of their time here on earth and simply doesn't have to be in opposition to the lives they are able to create for themselves.

The moment we start any dialogue about 'the box', whether we are *in it*, *outside of it*, or attempting to *crush it*, we can observe the inevitable temptation to use 'the box' as a means to create separation or pay homage to a hierarchy of *better than*. We've reduced an enormous group of Earthlings who are teaching or learning by using various religious, political or socio-economic states, adhering to certain doctrines, binding laws or traditions, down to those who are 'in the box' and those who are not. Admittedly, as a young adult with fire in her eyes and passion in her heart, a 'do-gooder' and crusader, so to speak, a lengthy maturation process preceded the realization that sometimes life's most educational moments can be found inside some of those boxes.

I have attempted to teach my girls that *they are who they are by their own design*, and to define this as *in* or *out* of any kind of box is a moot point, based solely on the understanding that every human being they encounter will have a different definition of 'the box'. By judging others as 'in the box' from our self-appointed stations somewhere on the outside, we are automatically suggesting that *our ways* are somehow more valuable or (r)evolutionary to the soul's journey. Can spirituality and free-thinking within an incarnation allow us to be more conscious? *Certainly.* More aware? *Absolutely.* More anchored in love? *Unequivocally.* More important to the dynamic and dichotomy of the soul's intent while on earth? *I would beg to differ.* In a world full of limitations and compartmentalisation, dogmas and blatantly discriminatory yet accepted social 'norms', watching two little girls grow, challenge, question and evolve as they unwrap the gifts that hide within an infinite supply of boxes, has been one of my paramount pleasures.

Why all of the talk about boxes? When contemplating how to approach this overwhelmingly personal chapter about grace as opportunity, an 'out of the box' moment, as described by my daughter's former primary school principal seemed appropriate. Jemma Skye was a precocious seven year old when we decided that although I am not Catholic nor religious and that she was new to the concept of choosing a spiritual or religious practice, she had the unique opportunity to educate herself from *inside the box* of the most predominant religion in Ireland, her country of birth. Excited by the prospect of a new white dress, patent leather shoes, a crown of baby's breath and in her case, what looked like a miniature Papal cape, Jemma embarked on the Irish tradition of making her First Holy Communion with all but a handful of kids in her class at St. Joseph's Primary School. A large portion of the second class curriculum involved memorising Bible verses, learning the parables of Jesus and reading about the events that led to the crucifixion of Christ. Having been exposed to paintings, books and statues I had collected from a variety of religious traditions from around the world, she was also no stranger to the Christian narratives. After all, I had been raised with them, myself.

One day, however, the phone rang, with the school's secretary requesting that I pay a visit to the principal. This, by now, had become a familiar routine. More than one teacher had endured the musings of my empathic eldest child who could see auras, spot manipulation or inconsistent behaviour a mile away and would drop a prophetic truth bomb because she just 'heard it in her head'. As one could imagine, primary school was quite the adventure for my kids.

On this particular occasion, the discussion in religion class had turned to the story of Judas and his betrayal of Jesus at the Garden of Gethsemane. For those who may not be familiar, the story goes that Jesus and the Apostles had gone to the garden to pray. Three times, Jesus asked his followers to remain awake and pray but instead, they slept. Eventually, he announced to the 'faithful' that the hour had come for him to be handed over to his enemies. This coincided with a ruckus created by a crowd of chief priests and Pharisees accompanied by a detachment of Roman soldiers, who had been led to the garden by Judas Iscariot, one of the nearest and dearest disciples of Jesus. Judas kissed Jesus on the cheek, the prearranged sign to the soldiers, that this was the person to be arrested. Jesus was brought off to stand trial before Pontius Pilot, the Roman governor of Judea. After committing what appeared to be the most infamous betrayal in recorded history, Judas ran away. Upon hearing news of the impending crucifixion of his most beloved friend, Judas first attempted to repay the silver he had been given in exchange for the whereabouts of Jesus. Consumed with grief and anguish, he ultimately took his own life by hanging.

On appearance, the story seems to be fairly cut and dry. A trusted friend is disloyal; a man undergoes unspeakable pain, ultimately losing his life because of it and the name Judas is forever remembered throughout the annals of time as a synonym for betrayal.

"Teacher!" Jemma's hand had apparently shot up like a bolt of lightning. "This whole thing is about Jesus dying for people's sins and then coming back to life. If that guy, Judas, hadn't done what he did, you wouldn't have a religion."

The impish grin splayed across the face of Principal John O'Neill as he relayed the story, is something I'll never forget. He had so enjoyed Jemma's antics over those past few years and had become a staunch supporter and ally. I must say, it ranks right up there with seeing the beautiful blonde toddler with the cheeky smile and sparkle in her eye, speak her first words or take her first steps.

For Jemma to contemplate, let alone *see* the bigger picture at the ripe old age of seven, was astonishing.

So why is this the perfect segue way for what I'm about to share? Very recently, I had the occasion to experience a betrayal and the opportunity to meet Grace at an intensely personal level. Quite frankly, it may be one of the most important experiences I've encountered in my own growth as a soul wrapped up in the mortal coil. I won't pretend for a moment that the initial shock didn't penetrate deep into the heart of my self-esteem...it did. Many years of consciously challenging myself not to react impulsively or from a space of victim mentality or fear, had created the perfect chance to see this betrayal and the Grace it could afford *me*, as a crucial application of a lifetime of learning, *if I allowed it*. And folks, no matter how hurtful, how awful, how justified or how many times you could say 'yeah, but in my case...' there is *always* a choice.

A dear friend of many years came to my office for a chat not long ago. He was anxious, visibly shaken and the anguish in his eyes spoke volumes before he ever uttered a word. He began by apologising profusely for the pain he knew he was about to cause me. He had been sitting with a secret for the last two months that by his description, was now making him physically ill. A mutual friend, and someone I had been incredibly close to for well over a decade, had written a text in attempts to dissuade this man from seeing me in a professional capacity for a healing session. Rather than simply saying that maybe we weren't a good match or that possibly a different avenue might better suit his needs, this very close and trusted friend had gone for the jugular. Her words were harsh and cruel and the depictions of my character were venomous and degrading. The last two lines were the most difficult to swallow. "So why is she in my life? Keep your friends close and your enemies closer."

I immediately thought back to all of the good times we'd had together. The laughter, the inside jokes, the intimate stories and delicate subject matter shared in complete trust, over cups of tea or when hanging out in my office; the adventures with our children over the years. The memories came flooding in like iron-clad battleships refusing to allow the shallowness of her comments to occupy and take over the special place she held in my sinking heart. The man before me was actually in tears. He knew how close this friend and I had been but he said he couldn't continue to sit back and watch her make a fool of me this way. He was truly distressed and in pain himself, because even more so than me, he too, had trusted this woman and took her betrayal to heart. When he had been vulnerable and in need of help, this was how she had responded. He found the split nature of her personality when around me and when talking about me behind my back, very disconcerting. He was now concerned about the safety of personal information which he had shared in confidence with this woman over the years. I thanked him for his courage and for valuing me enough to make me aware. My heart really went out to him. I can't imagine the distress he must have felt each time he saw my friend and me laughing and chatting, with me none the wiser.

Human nature kicked in and a highlights reel began to play out in my mind, as if on fast-forward. The exchanging of gifts at Christmas, the phone calls, the work I had sent her way because of my deep belief in her talent and authenticity. I let it play out. I didn't try to go all *'holier than thou'*, pretending that I wasn't wounded. Eventually, I picked my jaw up off the floor and began to recover from the initial shock and longing to disbelieve. I allowed myself to sit for a couple of days with the grief. I knew it was real because the desire to run off and tell everyone we both knew of how she had betrayed me simply wasn't there. Gossip felt like a mortal enemy. My heart genuinely ached. I knew that the distinct possibility existed that the man who had come to me may not have been the only person with whom she had expressed this opinion of me. It turns out, he wasn't the only one. Personal feelings aside, this was now professional slander. I realised very quickly, however, that the only way her comments could have any impact on my reputation or the work I do is if I allowed them to. After all, I had years of positive results to prove the efficacy of my work and knew plenty of people who had benefited...

Nope...that didn't feel right either.

That was my ego attempting to jump into the mix. I allowed ego to come along for the ride but it did not get a vote as to how I would deal with this situation. For a period of three days, I adopted the same metaphor of the betrayal, death and resurrection that can be found in nearly every ancient religious belief system from the Egyptian mythology of Isis and Osiris to the story of Jesus and Judas in the Christian Bible. Once I applied it to my current state of affairs, I went deep within. I had the chance to meet one of my most disturbing flaws face to face. In the past, whenever I felt that I had been forced to make a move as the result of what I perceived as someone else's bad behaviour, I had become angry; indignant that I had been 'forced' to change tack, respond accordingly or create a new boundary because someone had needlessly, senselessly caused a rift in the steady current of our relationship. In the past, I had chosen to see the injustice rather than the opportunity. Because of this, I knew that this was a true, tangible moment of Grace...not the *'aren't I just so spiritual and wonderful'* kind of Grace towards the one who deceived me, but the intervention of the immeasurable power of a love so Divine, a force that opens up channels of forgiveness and understanding despite my short-sightedness, that might otherwise have not been available.

That's the Grace that visited me on the third day. How did it find me? I had allowed myself the time to sit quietly with the sting, the foolishness I felt, the self-deprecation of having been so blind-all of the feelings and derogatory thoughts that accompany a good old fashioned self-flogging. I sat with them. On the third day, I simply said "Enough."

It was then that Grace came knocking at the door of my slightly shattered heart; what this trusted friend had done for me, not to me. This *Anam Cara*, or 'soul friend' as it's called in Irish, had given me one of the greatest occasions for growth in all of my fifty years. Whether her human avatar was conscious of this gift or not, is of great significance to her story of personal growth, but inconsequential to mine. My job was to receive this opportunity and use it to make adjustments to my life, not to condemn the one who presented it on a silver platter; a classic *don't shoot the messenger* scenario. She was carrying out a soul plan agreement that would allow me to see, feel and experience Grace so intensely, that I would be compelled to turn around and share the importance of the lesson. Think about it. If she hadn't been so close, so valued, so trusted, so loved, would it have made the same impact on me?

I sit humbly before you as I say that I am changed for the better because of her actions, not because I'm so wonderful, so forgiving, so spiritually advanced or so evolved, but because I had the bless-ed good fortune to be just barely coherent enough in my sorrow to allow a sliver of light through the door. That light then expanded in to one of the most valuable *and most difficult* challenges given to humankind; the chance to sit with oneself, feel a plethora of emotions and then rise out of the fear and pain and like a phoenix from the ashes. Instead of pitching a tent and setting up camp in the hurt and negativity or becoming a casualty of circumstance, I was able to become the grateful recipient of the Grace that is available to us all when our genuine, heart-felt intent is to truly let something go. This event gave me an up close and personal experience of the incredible phenomenon of Grace, and the capacity to implement years of developmental tools to understand it, perhaps for the very first time.

When my agent read this chapter, she immediately emailed me and said,

"So…what happened?!?! You know they'll all be wondering!"

The truth is that this chapter is what happened. I decided that rather than put my friend on the spot, to potentially shame or humiliate her, or in turn, create a space where excuses or backtracking might distract from ownership and accountability, that I would write to her. You have just read exactly how I chose to handle it. I feel that I have been given the privilege to be a force of love in this woman's life that may just allow her to move beyond the obvious hurt, damage and pain that would allow her to behave this way. We've all been or will be this woman at some point in one of our lives. Former First Lady, Michelle Obama, has said of the naysayers in her life, "When they go low, we go high." I'll take it one step further. The only reason we know how to go high is because we've risen from the ranks of those who go low. In you, I see me, and in all things, I see We.

Guruselum

Not long ago, my friend, Ilona, and I were discussing the concept of gurus. Those who have heard me speak or read any of my material would be quite familiar with my feelings on the subject. I really believe this world is not in need of another guru, be they self-proclaimed or instated by the masses. By its Sanskrit definition, a guru is a teacher, guide, expert or master. In today's culture of icons and pop stars, the term, guru, seems to have taken on a different meaning, fuelled by fame, fortune and how many followers they have on Instagram and Twitter.

A guru may be defined as an expert or master, but a great teacher and guide does not necessarily have to be a guru. As Ilona so simply put it, "Whenever a person follows a guru they are at risk of putting some aspect of their own personal responsibility on the shoulders of another." Wise, wise words, Ilona...

Expectations can run high and placing that kind of responsibility on another human can get tricky. In addition, it can leave an individual with a false sense of security and a tendency to shirk the extraordinary personal revelations found inside of accountability. I've always said that if someone is incarnate on Earth, it is because they are here to learn and grow. I've also been known to say that if someone is walking through this world, part of the package means being screwed up on some level. It seems a planet that is the proverbial schoolhouse for personal growth would require its inhabitants to be in search of illumination. I wouldn't even be a hundred per cent convinced that the 'masters' of the past were here solely due to altruism. The symbiotic exchange of energy and knowledge are trademarks of the earthly experience, leading me to believe that no one comes here without learning something... *not even the masters*. At the end of the day, each of us is sharing our own personal piece of the whole *with* the whole. If we can remain acutely focused on the organic manifestation of monumental lessons in everyday life, from the co-worker, the bus driver, the sibling or life partner, rather than constantly looking to a guru, I think we stand to have a much richer experience of what life has to offer.

We love to deify and worship those who seem to 'have it all together' a bit better than we do. Religious institutions draw in the crowds through deity or guru worship. Business moguls encourage eager young entrepreneurs to follow the leaders with the big ideas; the ones that lead to big bucks. All too often, those who seek to improve themselves get swept up in the notion that following the trail blazers will bring them one step closer to a successful or more meaningful life. The irony is that the very individuals in whom the faithful place their trust, most likely became self-actualized by dancing to the beat of their own drum.

In truth, offering one's gifts in order to help another *understand their way back to health* can feel a bit like learning you have just won the lottery while standing in front of a firing squad. *Sometimes* it can mean heartless ridicule, *other* times it can mean becoming the never ending dumping ground for people's anger and frustrations. For me, it is always accompanied by an indescribable awe at the unwavering awesomeness of the Multiverse of life's possibilities.

Commitment to a life of helping others to heal is not for the faint-hearted. Not long ago, I sat with a friend who is dealing with a debilitating neurological disorder and listened to him vent his rage at a God that would allow him to suffer when he had '*done all the work*' to heal himself. When I got into my car after listening, then talking him through his fury, there was a message on my phone from a woman in another country who was nestled in a hospital bed next to her dying husband; a recently vibrant man who had literally wasted away in front of her eyes. She was there, in his final hours, sending me a selfie of the two of them, expressing her deepest gratitude for the many chats we'd had over the last few months.

While she was so distressed by his imminent departure, she had found peace in understanding the *why* behind his soul's plan to exit the Earth plane at that precise time. He was 32. Her strength was awe-inspiring. Simultaneously, there was another message from a guy whose nine year old nephew had suffered a massive brain injury. He wanted to know if the child was going to make it or not.

In that moment, the answer was yes. After doctors frantically exhausted their resources trying interventions that ultimately the young boy's body could not handle, *yes* turned to *no* and he did not make it. This man was devastated, furious and lashed out at me, *because he knew he could*. When I say the life of helping others to find their own healing is not for those with a thin skin, I don't say it lightly. All of this happened in a matter of minutes, none of them realising that behind the scenes, in that same twenty-four hours, my own life was dramatically playing out. A dear friend had just joyfully announced her pregnancy, my mother had been critically ill, both of my children were struggling at school, one missing weeks of study due to pneumonia. I was happily weary from late nights of writing, unable to sleep while listening to my child cough from the depths of her soul. Recent blood work had revealed a serious personal health crisis that would need my immediate attention. Believe it or not, I wouldn't have changed a thing about that perfect storm. It's probably the main reason I signed up for these circumstances in this lifetime. Talk about a smorgasbord of highs and lows all at once! A life of service often means that people forget that the one who is serving is also surfing a tidal wave of emotional challenges. What better way to turn the tide of one's own tribulations than to share in the rich and raw experiences of another? It's also the best way to learn to shift out of a victim mentality.

For me, to feel a vast array of emotions all together without cracking under the pressure is what living is all about. For others, it might seem like an absolute nightmare. To be thanked profusely, to be dumped on, to be blamed, to have witnessed miracles, to feel inadequate, to have shared joy, to have been mistaken, to be right on target, all at the same time; I choose it…I also chose to come back here following my accident for **all of it**. I truly embrace the idea that my soul came here to push this physical form to its limits.

Understanding this concept can create an entirely different life experience, one that a huge portion of the population has forgotten is available. Imagine living in the knowing that every single event, every last morsel, every fear, every elation, *every everything* is of your own doing. Knowing this doesn't make someone a guru, because this knowing is available to anyone who is ready to remember it.

If I had a penny for every time someone has asked *Why Me,* I could pave my way to the Great Beyond in copper. Well, why not you? What is it that leads us to believe that we are not **entitled**, and yes, I mean **entitled**, to feel and experience *all* things on tap? In all of my years of service, no one has ever asked *Why Me,* when full of the joys. We seem to reserve that question for the tough times, the darker emotional states or the painful and traumatic physical challenges. Again, it appears that so many have reserved a sense of entitlement to the pleasurable state of mind. Most don't even pay attention to the fact that the dichotomy is always present, but when, for example, a person is newly in love, or the recipient of a better, higher paying job, the focal point of their attention has merely shifted towards the positive stimuli.

WHY DO PEOPLE DO THAT?

Simple. Because it *feels good* and we, as a species, have fooled ourselves into believing that if it *doesn't feel good*, it isn't an essential component of our growth and development.

What if the big "A-HA" is finding the potential for growth and expansion in all things? What if fear of the unknown was replaced with trust in your own plan? What if the sudden urge to melt down when the going gets tough was replaced with the desire to sit with the emotion, to allow it to wash in, feel it fully and then wash away as naturally as the outgoing tide?

There is the question of the man who cursed a Universe that would allow his nine year old nephew to die so suddenly;

robbed, he protested, of the opportunity to live a *full* life. He said he could deal better with the death of someone who had at least been given the chance to grow up. The mother of the thirty-two year old whose death was so horribly torturous and cruel would beg to differ. Her adult child left a loving wife, two young children and a future full of possibilities. There is no *better* or *fair* amount of time to live or die. When we suffer a loss, it is real, personal and important in a different way to each individual involved. When one can accept that each soul has a perfectly mapped out game plan, involving intricate and infinite circumstances in order to achieve a desired experience here on Earth, time becomes irrelevant, right along with age. If we only approached ourselves and our life experiences with the trust, reverence and respect befitting a Master Creator, we would soon discover that we already are the gurus that we so enthusiastically seek.

In sharing what I consider to be some of the most intriguing examples of the broad spectrum of healings I have been so fortunate to facilitate, it is important to note that the 'wow factor' varies depending on the individual. The stories I have chosen for this book were a sampling of my favourite examples of the many unique ways in which relevant information can reveal itself in the course of a session or the personal experiences of your fellow humans. There have been countless past life scenarios where neither the individual nor I had heard of the person they 'used to be'. Maybe we were familiar with a location, the time period or even a past event tied to the lifetime, but by no means were they all names remembered in the annals of history. Although many have, every person who has come to me with a terminal illness hasn't miraculously walked out with a clean bill of health. Healing is about embracing the soul's plan rather than spinning your wheels trying to change it. A healing doesn't always mean a happy ending in traditional terms. A good healing means redefining what we value and understand as worthy of our attention while here on Earth. As I have tried to stress throughout, it isn't the past life itself, or the current challenges a person experiences that are most relevant. It's all about the feelings and the frequency created by these encounters...It's ALL about the feelings and frequencies and what we intend to do with them. They say you can't take it with you. Money, material objects, absolutely not, but a soul is constantly filling its tool box with lessons acquired in the form of frequency and raised vibration, and that absolutely *can* and *will* be taken home again.

God, Allah, Buddha, Brahma, Christ; any and all of the greats, really are a state of being; names given in an attempt to place a personality or boundary on the frequency of Pure Love. Understanding that the frequency of the Creators and Masters we worship or seek already reside within us, that Paradise is not a place but a vibrational state of consciousness, understanding this will open channels of Grace that can heal any thought process that we have manifested as a physical or emotional actuality. Not only is Understanding the New Healing, it is our personal ticket to maximum expression while here on Earth. Imagine the possibilities...

Epilogue

New King James Bible
James 2:14-17
(I am, after all, a preachers' daughter)

14 What does it profit, my brethren, if someone says he has faith but does not have works? Can faith save him? 15 If a brother or sister is naked and destitute of daily food, 16 and one of you says to them, "Depart in peace, be warmed and filled," but you do not give them the things which are needed for the body, what does it profit? 17 Thus also, faith by itself, if it does not have works, is dead.

Did you ever have a week, even two, maybe a lifetime that seemed to have a running theme? A period of time where the Universe appeared to throw caution to the wind, breaking its own rule of impartiality, providing blatant experience after experience to provide and perfect a certain set of lessons? Understanding faith and the works that go with it? Let's just say this theme and I are up close and personal.

I'm a big supporter of elbow grease, putting your money where your mouth is, walking the walk and talking the talk. I'm equally a fan of trusting that timing is everything and nothing all at once and that patience is, *sometimes*, a virtue. Eager as we are sometimes to prove through our actions that we are on 'the path to enlightenment', I have come to realise that more often than not, the 'works' required for faith might be more from the heart and mind rather than physical in nature.

My Dad once told me, "There are two kinds of courage. Many a man is capable of the heroic action on the spur of the moment, but it takes a man of supreme courage to go on to face something which may haunt him for days ahead and which by turning back, he could escape."

Faith without works is dead…. Works may just mean the courage required to trust that all is unfolding as planned, even if it hurts...a lot. Allowing oneself to trust that a Divine plan is at hand may just be more difficult than the action one presumes is necessary to carry out the deeds of good will. Work on the physical plane is only one leg of the tripod. As the passage states, it is, after all, faith without work(s) that is dead. Without the emotional and spiritual investment in a plan, the plan doesn't stand a chance.

The fear of failure or appearing foolish has prevented more great acts from coming to fruition than any lack of physical prowess ever did. What, I ask you now, are you actually afraid of? It's time to start loving the life you live; all of it. If you think you've been dealt a crap hand, go spend a little time thinking about someone else rather than wallowing in your own misery. Extend your heart, your empathy, and your deeds of kindness to another who is struggling. You may just be surprised to see how quickly your perspective can change when your own shortcomings are not the centre of your Universe. The quickest way to change the hand *you've dealt yourself*, is with Love.

Eternity, the Grand Forever, is right here, right now and found in the conscious intention with which you construct every Present Moment (because they are ALL present moments). This is the understanding that can heal the way you live and love from this day forward.

My deepest, heart-felt gratitude for the gift of your valuable time and attention to this book.
Until We Meet Again…

Shine On.

SINESMUSIC.COM

SINES is a multi-faceted union of music and technology that brings mood harmonizing sound to the modern world-promoting balance, engagement, creativity, relaxation, meditation, productivity and HEALING. Our music is tuned and composed using specific frequencies that engage and balance the natural states of the physical and energetic bodies of the human experience.

By listening to an audio reproduction of a brainwave state that corresponds with your desired mood you are able to bring your body and mind into that mood within minutes. Repetitive use of these frequencies can alter habitual brainwave responses by collapsing old neural pathways and constructing new ones that better reflect the desired state of Being.

The Sines project is the brainchild of Greg Papania, sound engineer and frequency specialist in Los Angeles, California. The collaborative efforts of Greg, Andrew Chapin and Bernardo Vidal are found throughout the Sines music library, in addition to the contributions of professional artists, songwriters, sound healing therapists and musicians. The Sines team consists of doctors, scientists, and Emmy and Grammy award winning composers. Dr. Mary Helen Hensley has been conducting field research with astounding results for the last few years. The science behind the frequencies can be found on our website.

Listeners can download and experience Sines music for their personal use. Full service music licensing for TV, film and web libraries is also available. Sines is a project that aims to harmonise every area of life from offices, theatres, schools, child care facilities, malls, stadiums, public transportation, greenhouses and water supplies to the Health and Wellness industry, such as the fields of Neurology, Psychology, Immunology, Meditation, Yoga and Energy Healing. We are well on the way to accomplishing our mission of enhancing the human experience, *one positive vibe at a time.*

Acknowledgements

This is the book I've always wanted to write. When "Promised By Heaven" was released in 2015, many of these stories were put aside and I was told by my publishers that they were for 'another book'. The idea was to introduce readers to my story and me, but the truth be told, I would not be me or have a story to tell without the incredibly significant relationships I have formed with the courageous souls I have written about in Understanding is the New Healing. The personal accounts found within these pages are a mere smattering of the thousands of people I have been so blessed to encounter over the years on a personal and professional basis. Each one has profoundly touched me, literally reinventing my own understanding of the human adventure and what it truly means to heal. I could write volumes, and most likely will, of the transformations I have been so blessed to witness as a metaphysician. For now, I thank each and every one of the dynamic individuals who were brave enough to allow me to share their experiences with you. These are the true healers; the heroines and heroes who have faced their darkest fears, their greatest challenges and emerged with authenticity and accountability and a willingness to place privacy and vulnerability aside in hopes that even one life might be changed.

To Patricia Scanlan, what better role model could a person have than you? Your guidance, encouragement and honesty have essentially shaped the writer that I continue to become. You have openly shared your years of knowledge gained from writing countless best-sellers and have taught me just how important it is to write from the depths of my soul. We have laughed until our sides ached, cried together in Joy and sadness, and we have solved the world's problems over many late night cups of tea in front of a roaring fire. You have always had my welfare and best interest in mind from the first day we met and the respite and love I have received from you throughout our friendship has allowed me the strength to keep going. I am often asked, "Who heals the healer?" You, my dear, are forever healing me with your genuine love and true friendship. You are my very best Waggie!

To Lisa, at Lisa Hagan Literary Agency, I give thanks every single day for that fortuitous moment when the Divine caused our paths to cross. Not only did I gain the knowledge and expertise of a hardworking, principled agent who categorically "gets" what our mission is about, I met a dear and most trusted soul friend who 'fits me like a glove'. The added benefit of the invaluable input of your amazing mother, Sandra Martin, a powerhouse in the literary world, strengthens our team and enhances the wonderful things we will be able to accomplish in the name of Love. It's all happening on Route 58, girls!

Never one to forget from whence I came, my lifelong gratitude goes out to Dr. Niall MacGiollaBhuí and Susan McKenna at Book Hub Publishing in, Galway Ireland. This is where it all began. No different than a child who is taught to believe that anything is possible, my literary aspirations took root, were nurtured and began to grow at the Book Hub office in the fields of Athenry.

To Simon and Schuster in New York, I thank you for taking a chance on me with "Promised By Heaven". This message of love continues to shine, gathering momentum and changing lives and will hopefully continue to do so for many generations to come.

To Maureen Duffley, you are my office manager by day and my life manager 24/7. Together since the first day I set foot on Ireland's shore in 1997, you have stood by my side through thick and thin. Only you and I will ever really know what incredible feats we have actually managed to pull off on a shoestring and a prayer. Like a mother, sister, confidant, life organiser and dear friend all rolled into one, you have always been the complete package for me. I can say without doubt, none of this would have been possible without the contributions and support you have selflessly made over the years. Thank you for never once leaving my side.

To Maire\u00e1d Conlon, what great fun you and I have had over the years witnessing the miraculous together. You have made possible so many of these sessions that I have written about with your incredible organisational and management skills. A dynamic duo, we have redefined the sublime through our sessions and workshops at Spirit One Seminars. I am eternally grateful for the time and dedication you have given to me and to our collective mission.

To Ilona Pflaumbaum, Antje Goldmann and Andreas Klose, you introduced me to your Germany and its beautiful people. Never in my wildest dreams did I expect to fall so deeply in love with this magical country. I can never thank you enough for the opportunity to regularly share my work in Potsdam and Berlin, two of the most unexpected joys of my life. Andreas, you have created a vibrant and loving space to heal and have welcomed me with open arms. Ilona and Antje, your mastery of the English language has allowed me to share these stories, word for word with my German family and friends.

To Dr. Joe Steiner, you uprooted your life in Hong Kong and moved to Ireland to join the Athlone Chiropractic Care team, giving me the space and peace of mind to go forth and share the good news. Physically, you keep me going with your loving care and skilled hands, emotionally you have been so kind; a trusted and dependable friend. I am ever so grateful that your mind and heart are so open that you were able to boldly take the risk to follow your dreams so that I could follow mine. Soul friends forever.

To Emer, Siobhan and Bridget, it is an absolute pleasure sharing air with you in the office that love built. You enhance the atmosphere with your gifts, knowledge and most of all, your good humor.

To Daryl, not a day goes by that you don't check in on me. You'll never know how much that means to me and on how many occasions your kind, funny and caring messages have kept me afloat.

To Kate Murphy, you have always been that special friend who would drop everything to come to my rescue. We have that groovy kind of love that is simply always there regardless of time or circumstance. You and Anna are true treasures in my life.

To Rosaleen West, you have helped me to understand why my mother has always had such a loyal and lasting friendship with her hairdresser. Your chair has been like a confidential confession box and your ability to listen without judgement has been one of the steadiest and most dependable relationships I've ever had. Our friendship has grown over the years and I truly thank you for always being there for me…always.

To V and E, knowing you, working with you and loving you both have been true highlights in my life. You have blessed me with clarity of purpose that will forever drive me through the toughest of times.

To Alison Ray, my soul sister of a thousand lifetimes, how grateful I am that we found one another again. You are the great connector, the facilitator of so many magical events and I am blessed to have you in my life. Distance or time mean absolutely nothing in our relationship and we work in perfect harmony towards the same goals. Your compassionate and caring nature is rare and the love you have shown to my children and mother will never be forgotten. We ARE family.

To Gary and Janice, without you, my work in Virginia Beach would have never happened. You opened your home and your hearts, shared your friends and your knowledge and made Virginia Beach a home away from home for my family and me. I look forward to a lifetime of adventures with you.

To Christi Morrissey George and the amazing bookstore worker bees at the Edgar Cayce A.R.E., you have championed my cause, from the launch of "Promised By Heaven" to "Understanding Is The New Healing", and have so lovingly supported my work without fail. I thank my Lucky Charms for you.

To the Edgar Cayce A.R.E. members and staff in Virginia Beach, you have embraced me from the first day I crossed your threshold. From the greeters who welcomed me, to the Egypt Group who first sponsored me, the Glad Helpers who prayed with me, the tech crew who bring me to life when I give talks, the audiences who support me and the administration who make it all possible, my heartfelt gratitude for the love and trust you have shown in my work.

To my Virginia Beach family and friends, you are an ever present beacon of shining light in my life. You are such an inspiration and I love each and every one of you for your unique strength, your invaluable support and the incredible joy you bring to my life.
To Peter Bedard, my brother from another mother, may we continue to love, laugh and create together, always pushing one another closer to the light. The love expanded with the addition of Nelson and our soul family continues to grow.

To Lew Graham, we have been working on this particular mission for well over 13,500 years. You'd think we'd be tired of it by now, but I suppose, one does not tire of the pursuit of truth and the dissemination of knowledge. My, oh my, what interesting lives in which we chose to create this time around! Life wouldn't be the same without your love-in or out of a body.

To my Angel*ica* in LA, you have lovingly opened your heart and home, providing the space for me to set up shop, camp out and create magic. Melodee, you too, have always shared your sacred space, your wonderful friends and your love so that I have a safe and nurturing environment in which to vibrate. Michelle and Roxanne and Shannon, your home, your friendship, your friends and your amazing food are always a highlight of our journey to LA. Yvonne, Steve, Elena, Isabela, JP, Alex, Jackie, Paige, Nikki, Linda, Gary, Gina and Catherine, I love knowing that the west coast of America is in the very capable hands of some of the finest light workers this planet has ever seen. We have so much creating to do!

To Gracie Odoms, you are the total package, darlin', stretching the depth and breadth of what the human form can offer, to its absolute limits. You, my dear friend, hold my deepest respect because you simply had the courage to be your truth. We are Family.

To Greg Papania, the time has returned, my dearest. Grooving with you to the symphony of the stars is an absolute pleasure. I can't even remember when you weren't part of my life. You are pure love and we are bound forever by our mutual weirdness. sinesmusic.com is taking our work to a whole new vibration! I can't think of anyone I'd rather do this with than you. Pure. Joy.

To Andrew Chapin, I love your open heart, your open ears and that beautiful smile. Your creativity adds depth to my soul.

To Donnie and Morgan Most, an unexpected friendship emerged from a 'chance' meeting in a jazz club. I love, honour and respect your journey and bouncing ideas off of your creative minds is an absolute joy. You both define tenacity in my book. I am ever so grateful to call you my friends.

To my Sandra, my beautiful cousin Nicki, my Hairoine Holly and all of the beautiful ladies at Reflections Salon and Day Spa, where else can you heal, sell books, revive with the world's best massages and therapies AND walk out with a killer haircut all in the same day? You are the bomb, girlfriends!

To Dr. Sheila O'Brien, Dr. Maryellen Stephens and Dr. Anne Jensen, nothing beats a posse of gals who get what you are trying to say because they, too, took the red pill. I'm so grateful that we can embrace the weirdness together! Thank you for always letting me bounce ideas off of your highly intelligent and gorgeous heads!

To Deborah Ayers Stanley, although I can no longer hug you in person, your energy is radiantly alive in my heart every day. Thank you for allowing me into the most personal moments of your healing journey and for being the epitome of what it means to transcend with pure grace. This entire book was written with you in my heart.

To Dr. Gina Ricci Muscarella, last year you asked me some serious and thought provoking questions that made me dig deep. With you in mind, I have attempted to answer them to the best of my ability; I thank you for reminding me exactly why I had to write this book. You had the courage to express out loud things that most people think but would never dare say. You will never know how much I love and admire you for that.

To Loic Jourdain and Mirjam Strugalla, I love our conversations and I look forward to creating magic on film with you. I am so grateful to call you my dear friends.

To David Flynn, you have been championing me as well as my cause for so many years. Thanks for your brilliant words and to you and Mary for always believing in me.

To Karen Reid, I have such deep respect and admiration for your ability to turn hellish moments into heavenly inspirations. I truly live in awe of you and so many of the topics we have discussed became the subject matter I knew that I had to include in this material. You have been a beautiful muse, my friend.

To my Athlone Musical Society family, I look forward each year to the love and laughter the musical season brings to my hectic life. There is no sound sweeter than the harmony of good friends.

To Aishling, Robyne, Lorcan and Poppy, the family with the best ATTITUDE ever! We've danced through life together for the last decade and I wouldn't have missed a beat of it!

To Martin Ward at Na Fianna, I appreciate your motivation and dedication to keeping my girls and me fighting fit. There's a lot of sitting involved when writing a book and you gave me realistic targets and goals, helping me to feel really good about the skin I'm in.

To the Henry family, you have been so dear to my heart from the day you started taking care of Jemma when she was just a baby. Even though she's taller than all of you now, Jemma, Jada and I will always look up to you and be forever grateful for being part of your family.

To Siobhan, Turlough, Jane, Chloe, Gary and Ben, I doubt you realise just how important your role in this book has been. By loving Jada and making her feel as if she is one of your own, I have had the comfort of being able to work and gather stories throughout Ireland, America the U.K. and Germany, knowing that my little Bird was safe in your care. I really couldn't have done this without you.

To Laura, Ned, Hannah, Sarah and Jessica, all I have to say to you is only for you… my life would look very different without your love and support of Jemma. My heartfelt thanks to the entire family.

To the best neighbours when we need you, AnnMarie, Dermot, Shane and Siobhan, there is nothing sweeter than knowing that next door always has your back. Mr. Peabody and Sherman would be lost without you, AM, and so would I! Without ever batting an eye, you have always been there for me. Dermot, you and Shane have always stepped in whenever we needed. You have made the life of this single mom so much easier. I treasure your support and friendship.

To my IANDS family, I thank you from the bottom of my heart for your support. You have given a global platform not only to my story, but to the extraordinary accounts of life beyond death of so many other humans. Your work is so incredibly important and I am so blessed to be part of it.

To Shannon Strickland Hornsby, many people look back at their time in college and think of the parties, the fun, maybe even a few classes as some of the best times in their lives. For me, I look back at the day I met you in 1987 at Coker College and marvel at the fact that all these years later, a die-hard Myrtle Beach babe ended up relocating to my hometown in Virginia, married to one of our besties from school and now the invaluable companion and carer, first to my father before his passing and now to my mother. Mom is vibrant, healthy and going strong because of you. How do you thank that? I guess the best way is to let the world know that you are the glue that holds it all together. I couldn't be in Ireland if it wasn't for you. My entire life story would be playing out very differently if you weren't exactly where you are. Lord knows I love my Momma, and to know that she is in your loving care gives me the freedom to BE. Beyond grateful for you and I thank the

Heavens that you and Roger found each other again! The ripple effect of your love has changed the landscape of the Hensley family.

It's hard to believe that I have lived in Athlone, Ireland for as long as I lived in my hometown of Martinsville, Virginia in America. To my friends and family in each location, you have been my anchors on both sides of the Atlantic, allowing me to travel back and forth, gathering, learning, growing and expanding. Thank you all for giving me the wings to fly.

To my dear, sweet mother, Momma Helen, our adventures over the last few years have been, without a doubt, some of the greatest times of my life. Watching you allow yourself to shift, change and continue to grow in your late 80's, is the greatest gift you could have given to me. When each and every one of these wild stories took place, you were always at the other end of the phone, without a moment's disbelief, cheering me on and holding my greatest secrets in confidence, the same way you have for the last fifty years. Whether we are watching a show on Broadway in New York, lounging on the Queen Mary in LA or eating barbeque at Pigs R Us in Martinsville, you make every moment special and have taught me the importance of celebrating everything. I love you more than words could ever say.

Finally, to my number one reasons, my daughters, Jemma Skye and Jada Pacifica. You have forged my character, challenged my mind, captured my heart and given me the strength to follow my dreams. It is for you that I make it my business to fill this world with as much love as I possibly can. When I disappear behind the laptop to write a book, rather than complaining or making me feel like I am neglecting you as a mother, you have both cheered me on and shown incredible maturity in your understanding of my overwhelming desire to help others. You are both my greatest source of inspiration, love and healing. I love you, my beautiful girls.